T0386670

Beautifully
CASUAL HOME

Beautifully
CASUAL HOME

Elegant interiors for relaxed living

JUDITH WILSON

photography by Polly Wreford

RYLAND PETERS & SMALL
LONDON • NEW YORK

SENIOR DESIGNER Megan Smith
SENIOR COMMISSIONING EDITOR Annabel Morgan
LOCATION RESEARCH Jess Walton
HEAD OF PRODUCTION Patricia Harrington
CREATIVE DIRECTOR Leslie Harrington
PUBLISHING DIRECTOR Alison Starling

First published as *Casual Living* in 2010.
This edition published in 2024 by
Ryland Peters & Small
20–21 Jockey's Fields
London WC1R 4BW
and
341 E 116th St
New York, NY 10029

www.rylandpeters.com

10 9 8 7 6 5 4 3 2 1

Text copyright © Judith Wilson 2010, 2024
Design and photography copyright
© Ryland Peters & Small 2010, 2024

ISBN: 978-1-78879-611-8

The original edition of this book was catalogued
as follows.
Library of Congress Cataloging-in-Publication Data

Wilson, Judith, 1962-
  Casual living : no-fuss style for a comfortable home
/ Judith Wilson ; photography by Polly Wreford.
-- 1st ed.
    p. cm.
  Includes index.
  ISBN 978-1-84975-041-7
  1. Interior decoration--Psychological aspects. I.
Wreford, Polly. II. Title. III. Title: No-fuss style for a
comfortable home.
  NK2113.W55 2010
  747--dc22
                                      2010020383

Printed and bound in China

contents

introduction

We all live our lives in different ways. Some of us rush around; others take time to stop and stare. We create our homes in many different ways, too. Some of us crave pared-down simplicity; others prefer a gently dishevelled environment. But in among the myriad variations, and whether we live in the country or the city, we all need our lives to run smoothly so that we get precious time to relax. Creating a home that supports easy, unencumbered living goes a long way towards making daily life run on well-oiled wheels. Imagine a home that is organized yet relaxed, functional yet comfortable, unfussy but also beautiful. That's casual living. Isn't that the perfect way to live?

This is a book to help make home life easy, while also showing how to put together a casual, breezy style. There is a simple mantra: make your home work hard for you, so you don't have to. First, ask yourself what casual living means to you? For a busy singleton, a low-maintenance home may be high priority, or is your requirement a family-friendly home that can be tidied in a trice? If you have a fast-paced, stressful lifestyle, what elements can imbue your home with a chilled-out ambience? But first of all, there's a dash of hard work to be done. You can't adopt a casual lifestyle without getting organized. Edit your possessions

ABOVE Plan a family home where frivolity can spill over – everyone will enjoy doodling on a blackboard in the kitchen.
OPPOSITE With sleek stainless-steel surfaces, open shelves and everyday essentials to hand, this kitchen seamlessly combines efficiency with style.

so the essentials are to hand, and consider how to streamline your home to ensure that each room is easy to live in, but delivers maximum efficiency for the ebb and flow of life.

Once armed with new thoughts, it's time to crystallize your style options. Section one, Casual Style, helps decide whether you want a laid-back, country interior, or a crisp yet relaxed urban look. We all have a natural style inclination, so tap into it by creating a mood board, using tear sheets of interiors you love.

Getting the style right creates the delicious illusion of casual living, but casual living also concerns everyday practicalities. So section two, Casual Elements, helps you make

ABOVE Big, bold, scaled-up proportions make daily life easier. In this country kitchen, deep drawers offer a practical twist on conventional cupboards. **OPPOSITE** Aim for purity of styling and comfort. In this city living room, the monochrome scheme and mixture of velvet, cotton/linen and wool textures create an inviting combination. The painting is by Duncan Pickstock.

a beeline for functional decorative choices at home. If everyday activities are easy – from household admin to cleaning up – arduous or mundane tasks can be quickly transformed into easy pit stops along the way. In section three, Casual Rooms, the focus is on bringing key rooms to life so that each one fulfils a dedicated function. A well-planned room, after all, means that you have more time to relax.

Whether adopting casual living involves big changes or minor tweaks, your goal is to achieve a balance between mental purity and an easy home life. Casual living is not about having a messy or disorganized home. Instead, it is about creating a practical, flexible, easy-care living space. If you create a home that will help life run smoothly, you can help yourself to a new way of living. Casual living is everything you need.

casual style

At its heart, casual style is a blend of easy furniture, soothing colours, no-fuss surfaces and textiles that clean up or shake out effortlessly, time after time. Keep things real: pick comfortable pieces and don't over-match for a look that's laid back and gently evolved, yet sturdy enough to withstand the rigours of daily life.

LEFT Look out for armchairs and sofas with a lazy, low-slung silhouette, which visually strike the right note as well as being comfortable. Play with accessories to create a chilled mood: in this relaxed hall, a painting is casually propped against the wall, while a chandelier in the grate adds sparkle to an empty fireplace. OPPOSITE Vintage fabrics are an ideal choice for country casual living, as they are already gently worn in. In this rustic sitting room, a Chesterfield sofa has been upholstered with a patchwork of old floral fabrics and damasks. Use accessories to emphasize the casual mood: here, a haphazard mix of photos, candles and vases creates a focal point. The dramatic seascape is by John Hamper.

country casual style

Laid-back comfort, gently faded textiles and distressed surfaces sit at the heart of country casual style. The look thrives on a deliberate jumble of well-worn furniture and mismatched accessories — easy pieces for effortless living. These are rooms that allow you to come home, light a candle or flop on the sofa, and relax.

OPPOSITE Distressed surfaces look perfectly at home in a country casual kitchen and are very practical, so aim for an interesting textural mix. In this family dining zone, a painted and gently peeling armoire is teamed with an old scrubbed pine table that has a blackboard-painted top.

LEFT If you have open shelves for stacking china and glassware, use them to multi-task. Add cup hooks for mugs and decorative accessories, and celebrate a relaxed rural lifestyle by filling glass cups or bowls with finds from country walks. **BELOW** In a busy family kitchen, a stand-alone sink is a useful addition, for an overflow of dirty dishes, arranging flowers or peeling vegetables. This salvaged find, bought on eBay, has been teamed with a splashback of European encaustic tiles. Choose utilitarian kitchen accessories to keep things real, such as a metal bin for recycling bottles.

All country dwellers know that rural living necessitates a certain casual style. The presence of animals and muddy boots, and the close proximity to the great outdoors, means that everything at home must be robust – even, perhaps, a little shabby. Traditional country style can be overly fussy, with florals and frills, or – at the other extreme – too utilitarian, low on comfort and style. The country casual style that works in today's world is a gently pared-back look that's child's play to maintain and – the real bonus – perfectly tailored to promote a chilled-out way of life. Even better, if you live in the city, but dream of green fields, it is easily adapted for a townhouse setting.

Establish the foundations of your country casual style by examining the architecture at home. Not all country properties are bristling with rustic features, but there may be a few distinguishing characteristics to spark an idea. An inglenook fireplace with an exposed brick hearth might prompt the use of other rough and ready surfaces, like battered leather and salvaged terracotta tiles. A kitchen boasting ancient beams might cry out to be accessorized with ladderback chairs, their design echoing the symmetry of the ceiling, and a table of rough planks. Or the sun-bleached painted exterior of a fisherman's cottage could inspire a colour scheme of pale seaside tones and distressed painted furniture.

RIGHT AND FAR RIGHT A single architectural cue can be the springboard for an entire scheme. The exposed brickwork in this kitchen has prompted a mix of a painted armoire, an iron chandelier, distressed zinc worktops and handles, and even a muted colour scheme. **BELOW** Pick tableware, from vases and serving bowls to everyday plates, to match a distressed, rustic theme.

All is not lost if your home lacks strong architectural features. Add new elements – but ensure they are reclaimed and already gently distressed – or 'age' brand-new materials so that they sit happily within a country property. Large surfaces, such as walls and floors, deliver the biggest impact, and instantly add rustic character. For floors, architectural salvage yards offer a vast choice of reclaimed floorboards, flagstones and terracotta or ceramic tiles. To recreate the mood of traditionally plastered walls, get a specialist to use lime plaster – it has a soft texture and a lustre that you won't achieve with modern finishes. If you're adding a new extension to an old building, chunky open shelves made from reclaimed timber or new storage using traditional panelled doors will add rustic character.

At the heart of today's country casual style is a crisp freshness, so be prepared to contrast the patina of age with clean new surfaces. For example, an old tessellated tiled floor could be teamed with pristine white-painted walls, or the deliberately rusty feet of a reclaimed claw-foot bath set against modern brick-style tiles. In a kitchen, you might team uneven original plaster walls with a smooth black rubber floor. Do

THIS PAGE In an easy country-style kitchen, an island unit is given a new twist: one side is fitted with open shelves facing the dining table. Use giant platters and baskets to store fruit and vegetables.

THIS PAGE Consciously play with textural variations, soft or hard, to reinforce a simple country mood. In this guest room, the mix of a handmade timber side table, stitched quilt, a framed tribal textile and sheer curtains creates a low-maintenance yet still cosy mood.

OPPOSITE CENTRE Extend the casual ethos to creating your own furniture. These simple side tables, made by the owner, were cut from fallen saplings blown down in a storm.

remember the practicalities, too. While the appeal of using reclaimed surfaces is that they are already gently worn and thus immune to the hurly-burly of everyday life, they must, like new surfaces, be easy to care for. Beware chipped tiles or cracked porcelain sinks, which will be time consuming to maintain.

Vintage surfaces provide a relaxed framework for country casual style, but the right colour scheme will perfect the look. For a subtle mood – and isn't that at the heart of casual living? – pick the nourishing shades of nature. Consider oatmeal, caramel and chestnut tones inspired by timber through to the knocked-back greys and off-whites of stone or stormy skies. Use these neutrals on floors and walls, but don't be afraid to play with them tonally, perhaps adding a very dark floor, or washing a ceiling with a mid-tone. Think about subdued tones for walls, from pigeon to straw. Some rustic surfaces will look marvellously fresh when teamed with white paint, but a softer off-white may

RIGHT In a guest bedroom, it's essential to have extra bedding. Here, spare blankets and pillows are piled into a basket.
TOP LEFT AND RIGHT Put together treasured accessories in simple arrangements so that they don't look self-conscious, and spice up neutral tones with flashes of colour. In a country bedroom, old shoe lasts have been nailed to the wall to create impromptu hooks.

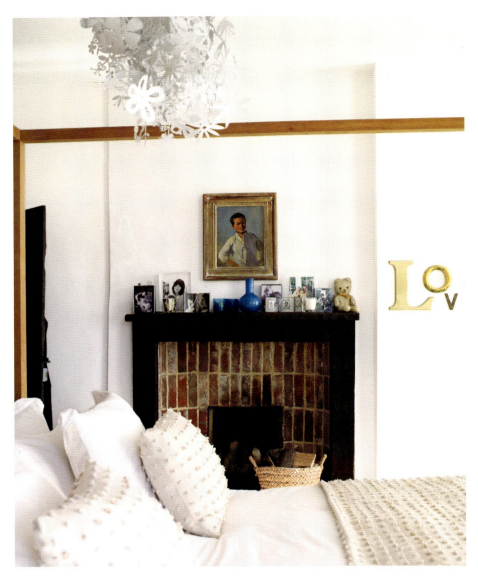

LEFT When planning an interior, consider the arrangement of the room. In this bedroom, the plain four-poster bed has been placed centrally, to maximize a great view, as well as providing freedom of movement.

BELOW Clothing that's in use on a daily basis can be integrated into a casual, simple decorative scheme. Here, second-hand shelves hold an array of shoes and are given a decorative twist with the addition of a painting and china dog.

be more appropriate in a property with less natural light. Trawl historic paint ranges, remembering that the inexpensive big-brand manufacturers have shades that are every bit as effective as designer ranges. Pick fun, zingy hues from nature for accent shades, from leaf greens to deep-sea turquoise, bright cherry and rosebud pink – an instant energizer, guaranteed to stop any interior looking too perfect.

Textiles to suit country casual style should be cocooning and warming. They also need to be durable. For a clean-cut look, opt for simple, heavy curtains, gathered onto a plain heading and hanging from a chunky wood or steel pole. Lined curtains keep out chills, and lining with a deep colour or a subtle striped cotton gives a fresh, crisp look. Appropriate curtain fabrics include heavy linen – look out for designs with a stripe reminiscent of vintage grain sacks – thick cotton, denim, wool or crewelwork. Hemp fabric also hangs beautifully. Casual country works best put together with a pared-down touch, so plains are the simplest choice, but bold weaves, like herring-bone, will add a twist of textural interest. For a softer take on the look, use a faded floral cotton or linen print, preferably a vintage one. If you use florals for curtains, however, go for plains elsewhere to keep things unfussy.

Casual living is as much about how you live as how your home looks. Plan the layout of each room to create a space that's easy to move around in and simple to maintain, as well as looking good.

THIS PAGE Pick bedding that looks good when carelessly ruffled so that the bed can be made with a quick shake. In this easy seaside room, seersucker sheets, a snug sheepskin and a soft quilt in leaf green provide an inviting contrast to the simplicity of the decor. The painting is by British artist Audrey Clark-Lowes.

home, broad striped deckchair cotton canvas with eyelet headings can be strung across a metal pole, or panels of traditional ticking gathered onto wooden dowels, for the most casual of window dressings. For a clean, simple look, invest in plantation or panelled shutters.

Your country casual home is the place to come in, flop on the sofa and relax, so upholstery fabrics must be tough. An antique sofa doesn't necessarily have to be re-covered. There is a charm to worn velvet or tapestry: it isn't pristine, so can be treated nonchalantly, and tattered chairs look relaxed teamed with vintage surfaces. Likewise, an old leather armchair is the perfect addition. If you do reupholster, consider patchwork upholstery: it is painstaking, but gives a whimsical new take on the rustic quilt. Using vintage fabric for reupholstery means it will already look gently worn in – an old sheet or second-hand chintz curtains, cut to size, are good options. Washable loose covers in linen or cotton work for a country casual mood; make them extra baggy to allow for shrinkage.

Country casual style is all about maintaining a laid-back lifestyle, so look out for easy furniture shapes that promote relaxation. Choose pieces that can be moved around at a moment's notice, from armchairs on castors to a timber top on a pair of trestles for a dining table. Casual style is the antithesis of a perfectly coordinated room. In the same way that the interiors in old, grand country houses evolve quite naturally, with inherited, borrowed and new pieces overlapping from one decade to the next, aim to mix and match styles to maintain a relaxed aesthetic.

Team curtains with simple blinds/shades, so that in summer you can take down the curtains or replace them with unlined drapes. For unlined curtains or blinds/shades, consider loose-weave linen sheers, cotton voile, lace or monogrammed vintage sheets. Check with the manufacturer or supplier that your chosen fabric can be machine-washed, or make up curtains after washing to avoid the shrinkage issue. In a seaside country

ABOVE Tailor the style of joinery to promote a pared-down yet rustic mood. In this tiny sitting room, shelves allow for a casual display, yet closets hide clutter and everyday technology like the DVD player. The painting is by Audrey Clark-Lowes.

LEFT Become a magpie, and pick up shells on walks, or old postcards in junk stores.
BELOW Pared-down surroundings emphasize decorative treasures. Indonesian shadow puppets, a seascape by French artist Ed Mandon and family photos create a simple still life here.

Although traditional furniture shapes are particularly suited to country style, from a buttoned Chesterfield to a deep Knole sofa, don't be afraid to add contemporary pieces. Shiny metal kitchen chairs add a new dynamic to a scrubbed pine table, as will a modern four-poster bed mixed with a distressed French armoire. Just because furniture is vintage doesn't mean it can't be super-efficient. A rustic linen press in a bathroom, for example, can be lined with Perspex boxes to keep toiletries in check, while old apple crates, nailed in a grid onto a dining wall, create the ultimate casual open shelving.

As for accessories, the key to country casual style is to indulge in easy pieces that will cocoon and inspire you, but not add clutter. Think of placing your accessories in a new way: instead of hanging a picture, prop it; instead of folding a blanket over a chair, toss it; pile books, rather than lining them up. To earn their place in the country casual interior, accessories should be ever-changing. If you love to be surrounded by family photos, mix them up in a combination of frames, tucked into a mirror or tacked straight onto the wall. Use the great outdoors as a rich source of decorative inspiration, whether it's a branch of spring blossom on the mantelpiece or a newly gathered pile of seashells on the kitchen table. Gather, touch, enjoy – that's the spirit of casual living.

LEFT A clear-cut layout and a dynamic yet practical colour scheme lie at the heart of this city family home. There is minimal furniture to impede traffic flow, and the slim runner takes the eye straight to the heart of the house. Yet the moody tones of the wall and the sofa upholstery cleverly link the hall and open-plan living room. Deliberately use the odd exuberant shade to keep things casual, and remind everyone that city living is stimulating. The abstract landscape entitled April Pond is by Irish painter Sean McSweeney. **OPPOSITE** Distressed surfaces work well in an urban setting. In this pared-down city apartment, a utility-style coffee table, bleached floorboards and Southeast Asian artefacts reflect the textures and shades in the painting by Thai artist Thaiwijit Puangkasemsomboon.

city casual style

Crisp silhouettes, a confident palette and a thoughtful approach to space planning form the backbone of city casual style. Match design choices with your natural preferences, from raw industrial to streamlined chic. Take a light-hearted approach that encompasses softness and a sense of fun so your city space is a haven, too.

Pieces with linear or boxy silhouettes instantly impart a snappy city mood, but add the occasional curvy piece for softness.

THIS PAGE The enfilade of rooms in this city flat is potentially formal. Yet by deliberately mixing 20th-century classic furniture and lighting with a raw stone tabletop and cracked leather armchair, the owner has created a dressed-down mood.

LEFT City rooms need to be multi-functional, so keep key zones clutter free. In this airy dining space, the oval table, teamed with classic Eames chairs and salvaged pendant lights, provides space for quick suppers, a spot to work or somewhere to pull up a chair and read. BELOW Arrange furniture and lighting so that every room is ready to go the second you get home. In one corner of this sophisticated city apartment, a relaxing sofa, a perfectly angled lamp and a side table create a welcoming reading spot. Clean-cut, linear furniture shapes are perfect, but for a glamorous twist, pick upholstery and accessories in neutrals or soft pastels. The painting is by Danish artist Malene Landgreen.

Weekday city living can be hectic and time pressured, with long hours spent away from home. When the weekend comes, relaxation should be your highest priority, not tidying up. So creating a streamlined interior in a city home is vital. Many urban dwellers compromise on the size of their living space in order to enjoy the buzz of city life. Therefore, managing your space is crucial, too. Long before thinking about the visual cues of city casual style, address the basics. Your living space must be easy to move around in, well organized and simple to keep tidy on a daily basis. But it must also be relaxing; a sanctuary to come home to.

Your interpretation of city casual style will be affected by the architecture at home. For example, a converted loft, with concrete floors and metal-framed windows, will call for harder-edged decorative elements, from a zinc-topped kitchen

island to outsize enamel lamps. By contrast, an apartment in a period townhouse, with elaborate mouldings and a pretty fireplace, might inspire an elegant scheme featuring velvet, pale colours and marble. What attracts you about the city? If it's surfaces like metal or brick and a monochrome palette, look for furniture and finishes to develop into a full-blown scheme.

Choose hard surfaces, from walls to floors, according to whether you want to go grittily urban, or elegantly urban. Original floorboards can be used as the basis for either look – and wood flooring cleans up well with a quick

ABOVE LEFT Teamed with the right furniture and surfaces, sombre urban hues, from graphite to ash, can be interpreted in a comfortable way. In this family sitting room, the curves of the sofa with the retro lighting fitting, and the textures of the shagpile rug and velvet cushions, create a simple yet sophisticated retreat. **ABOVE** Group ceramics and pottery in a haphazard manner, mixing heights and shapes, rather than creating a formal display.

THIS PAGE In this city kitchen, grey-painted bricks, classic aluminium chairs and steel doors create a crisp and utilitarian look, yet the warmth of the wood table and shelf unit helps to maintain a friendly family ambience.

THIS PAGE A city bedroom proves that it's possible to maintain comfort with a pared-down, casual style. Fluffy duvets/comforters are easy to shake out, while ethnic cushions and vibrant art inject personality. The black and white photograph is by Morten Bjarnhof.
OPPOSITE BELOW RIGHT With its heavily patinated surface, a vintage office storage unit sets a city casual style, yet is also immensely practical for holding clothes. A low-slung leather chair adds softness.

FAR LEFT A beautiful item of clothing can look wonderful as an integral part of the decoration. In this room, a summery pleated frock, suspended from a plain metal coathanger, creates an impromptu display.
LEFT Use shoes, beads or handbags to similar effect. Loop your necklaces on a radiator or around a dressing-table mirror, or toss footwear into a giant wicker basket.

vacuum. Lightly sanded and waxed, with scuffs intact, boards suit an edgy city look, but painted in a dark colour, like graphite, or treated with Swedish lye soap, they look sophisticated. Polished concrete, limestone slabs, slate and rubber floors also give a streamlined effect, and are low maintenance. Underfloor heating, great for going barefoot, is the ultimate investment for casual living. As well as plain matt paint, other wall choices are polished plaster, painted brick or a feature wallpaper, provided you stick to a simple, graphic pattern.

Choose the colour scheme while working on the hard surfaces, as concrete or polished plaster form the basis of a scheme anyway. Think of an urban landscape and your city casual mood board instantly features neutrals – grey, chocolate, black, white. Grey is a versatile choice: it can be pretty as a pale tone, but chic and practical in a darker tone. Consider a charcoal wool sofa in a casual family home – it ticks all the boxes. Black and white is a smart combination, easy to accessorize with other colours. You only have to think of the neon advertising hoardings on any city street or the flash of blue sky in between tower blocks to know that bright shades work well with neutrals.

shelves or glass-fronted cabinets come in marvellously distressed finishes. Freestanding furniture is also an option. A distressed painted shelf unit, crammed with china, is both casual and elegant. Ensure that storage works for you – the ultimate test is how quickly you can find things or put them away.

Key furniture pieces, from sofas to beds, must work hard so that the living environment stays uncluttered. Look into multi-functional pieces, from an ottoman with concealed storage to a purpose-built headboard with integral shelves. Pieces with linear or boxy silhouettes instantly impart a snappy city mood, but add the occasional curvy piece for softness. Whether you choose modern or period furniture is up to personal inclination – an artless mix gives a particularly chilled-out mood. The odd vintage piece, such as classic 20th-century dining chairs, looks edgy, but team with comfort, too, like a big squishy sofa and a well-sprung bed. Pay attention to materials and finishes. Modern furniture often comes in high-tech surfaces such as toughened

Life is hectic in the city, but it's also exciting. So while it's up to you to create a living space that's soothing, rooms should also have a dash of the unexpected.

Vibrant shades – chartreuse, scarlet, aubergine – will instantly enliven a room, but don't overdo it. One red leather armchair, paired with grey walls and a black floor, has a chilled-out appeal. Wall-to-wall primary colours do not.

Lack of space is often a pressing issue, so storage needs early thought. Custom-built shelves and closets can be a lifesaver in terms of organizing your life and keeping your living space uncluttered. Use every spare alcove, or devote an entire wall to storage. For an edgier look, flush-fitting closet doors can be faced with galvanized steel, birch-faced ply or high-gloss spray paint. For a sophisticated mood, use wood veneer, painted MDF/fiberboard or mirrored doors. Save unfitted storage, particularly vintage pieces, for an edgier style. Metal factory

ABOVE Tailor your storage: in this master bedroom, a purpose-built headboard creates a clever division behind the built-in wardrobes and the room itself. A painting by Irish artist Cormac Healy adds a strong focal point. **RIGHT** Have fun with colour: in this all-white 1960s house, a jumble of retro glass in different shades of green enlivens a staircase window.

THIS PAGE Custom-made storage is a worthwhile investment: count and measure key items so that there is a home for everything, and keep the style plain and simple. Interesting details, such as these subtle cut-out handles, look smart.

glass, lacquered acrylic or powder-coated steel, which wipe down in a trice. Have fun mixing and matching with vintage finishes, from rusty metal to distressed painted wood.

City living doesn't preclude comfort: if anything, it is even more important to cocoon yourself. The shortest cut to comfort is to pick city-smart but easy-care upholstery fabrics that feel luxurious. Opt for an upholstered sofa in a touchy-feely fabric that won't crease, such as jumbo cord, wool, chenille or horsehair. Or, pick a textured fabric, such as nubbly wool or velvet, that looks deliberately rumpled. Leather, antique or new, is easy-care. If you choose your upholstery fabrics from a neutral palette, add other upholstered pieces in bright accent shades. If you've gone for a grittier look, then simple cushions in vintage fabrics or denim are practical choices. For a more elegant city casual look, pile the sofa with a cashmere throw and cotton velvet cushions.

City window treatments must look fabulous, control light and protect privacy. Think through a busy weekday morning – you should be able to raise blinds/shades in a millisecond and pull curtains with minimum fuss, so ensure that they are well made. Simple, unobtrusive roller blinds/shades always look smart, especially in a city space with fantastic mouldings or high ceilings. Roman blinds/shades are more elegant, but choose a crease-free fabric like cotton canvas that will pull up into neat pleats. Curtains need to be simple, full length and with a good drape. Medium-weight linen, brushed cotton or wool always look smart. Just because you are going simple doesn't mean

ABOVE This chic bedroom treads a fine line between the crispness of city pinstripes and a black and white palette, and a distinctive softness. Easy, natural textures set the tone, from natural linen slipcovers to cotton bedding. Yet it is the owner's collection of female portraits and photos, simply propped on custom-built shelves, that stamps a feminine and welcoming ambience.

you can't add detailing. An edging in a contrast colour or subtle pin-tucking at the base looks relaxed and chic. Hang curtains from plain wood or metal poles with rings or eyelets.

Choose and display accessories to create the illusion of more space. Don't overcrowd, but don't be too minimal either. Keep potential display areas, such as the mantelpiece or a console table, uncluttered – leaving room to add a budding twig snipped in the park or a postcard just bought from an art gallery. Have fun with artwork. Rather than hanging several small pictures on each wall, experiment with one giant painting and keep other walls bare for a pared-down look. Other casual options are a ceiling-hung mobile or the odd piece of sculpture on the floor. You are aiming for a chilled-out mood rather than a stiff look-but-don't-touch rule.

Life is hectic in the city, but it's also exciting. So while it's up to you to create a living space that's soothing, rooms should also have a dash of the unexpected. Use sensory tools to enliven every room, just as the city streets inspire you. Fresh flowers, a scented candle or uplifting music will bring city rooms to life.

ABOVE AND LEFT Raid your wardrobe for the prettiest items and keep them out on show. Aim for a deliberate mix of formality and whimsy. Here, a sophisticated antique chest of drawers is accessorized not only with attractive perfume bottles but also a simple canvas director's chair and casual ropes of necklaces. **RIGHT** Use vintage bowls or pots to keep smaller accessories in order.

casual elements

Choose beautiful, practical and long-lasting elements to create the framework of your living space, and you're in for an easy ride. Tailor choices to your own style preference and lifestyle, but remember that soft colours, low-maintenance surfaces and efficient storage are always the backbone of a casual living home.

easy colours

Swathes of colour on walls, fabric or furniture attract our attention and affect our mood, so pick shades to which you are intuitively attracted. Get the colours right, and they will imbue a room with creative energy. A casual interior should also be a fun space, so move out of your comfort zone and experiment with shades that relax and inspire you every single day.

LEFT AND ABOVE LEFT Your colour palette should encompass not just walls, upholstery and floors, but accessories, too. In a room where there are dominant features, such as the panelling and parquet in this sitting room, pale creamy tones are a crisp, easy choice and pull the room together. The painting is by Andre Vogt.

ABOVE CENTRE AND RIGHT Sludgy neutral shades tend to be the forgotten cousins of the colour spectrum, but they are unbelievably versatile. Pale or dark taupes, bones, greys or mushrooms look gentle and moody on their own, yet appear more dramatic when contrasted with clean, bright white.

THIS PAGE Vibrant colours are joyful to live with, but need careful handling. In this sitting room, the florals and scarlet shutters work so well because the colours are clearly defined on the sofa and windows; the floor, walls, furniture and accessories have been kept subtly neutral.

THIS PAGE There is a reason why art gallery walls are white. Pure white walls are useful tools for directing attention towards a collection of simple yet beautiful decorative items. In a corner of this tranquil bedroom, glass-fronted boxes filled with nature's treasures become a focus of delicate pattern. Subtle contrasting wallpaper has been used to soften the starkness of the white paint in the bedroom.

OPPOSITE By painting walls, ceiling and flooring white, you can create an utterly versatile space, where accessories and furniture can change on an almost daily basis. In this light-filled dressing area, bright patchwork pouffes add quirky pattern and colour.

White is an obvious choice for those wanting an easy-come, easy-go interior, and for good reason. White provides a clean canvas for showing off multi-coloured accessories, it goes with everything and it can look modern or rustic, depending on the surfaces with which it is teamed. Yet pure white can also be stark, and it is a misconception that wall-to-wall white paint creates the most relaxed interior. In fact, it's kinder on the eye to choose softer off-whites, from milk to silver grey or ice blue. Some paint ranges offer graded whites, so you can use a different shade for ceiling, walls, woodwork, floor and skirting/baseboard, giving the room definition and warmth. Play with surfaces to create a mix of shiny and matt. Glossy white floorboards or ceramic tiles can look cold, but will easily soften when teamed with contrasting white textures such as a translucent porcelain light fitting or a shagpile rug.

Gentle grades of true colour are the easiest way to imbue your home with a chilled-out mood. Using subtle shades takes courage, but pays dividends – used confidently throughout they add individuality, and pale shades look terribly chic. Choose sludgy pastels, such as mushroom pink or lichen grey-green, or really soft versions of fresh colour, like pale olive, plaster pink or lavender. Muted shades won't look very exciting as a tiny paint swatch or fabric cutting. Yet hold that same

swatch against a bright green leaf and you will see the colour come alive. Once painted on a wall or used as upholstery, these shades become deliciously chameleon-like, bleaching out in bright sunshine and deepening as dusk falls. They look

It's kinder on the eye to choose softer off-whites, from milk to silver grey or ice blue.
Some paint ranges offer graded whites, so you can use a different shade for ceiling,
walls, woodwork, floor and skirting/baseboard, giving the room definition and warmth.

crisp teamed with white, so are breezy choices in a bathroom, but practical when mixed with darker shades, perhaps plum or chocolate, in a working kitchen. Don't be afraid of colour: it's a joyful way to sharpen up your living space.

Casual living may be about being bright and breezy, but dark shades, such as black, grey, indigo and ink, also have a place in the casual home. Whether used for upholstery or paintwork, deep tones are super-practical, especially in a family space. Use them sparingly though. On cabinetry, on architectural mouldings, such as door or window frames, or on features like radiators, they will neatly highlight the crispness of white and provide visual get-up-and-go in a busy household. A section of wall painted in a moody shade can define a tranquil area in an open-plan space, and dark-painted floors are both deeply practical and – particularly in a city casual space – look either sophisticated or urban, depending on the way they are accessorized.

ABOVE In this funky city kitchen, black is used confidently as a defining colour. Victorian display cabinets have been repainted in black lacquer, and family photos are displayed in matching black frames.
RIGHT AND FAR RIGHT Soft neutrals like biscuit or steel are less harsh than pure white with antiques or paintings.

THIS PAGE When particular pieces of furniture are key to a room scheme, use their innate colours and textures to guide you when choosing a wall shade. In this relaxed dining room, the bleached floorboards, plywood chairs, painted tabletop and antique mirror are all in varying yellowy timber tones. A pale biscuit wall paint works gently with those colours.

THIS PAGE In this chill-out sitting room, brilliant colour has been used with a confident hand. Colour needs to be punctuated to stop it being overpowering: in this case, the giant canvas by Thai artist Attasit Pokpong lightens the blue wall, while heavy buttoning on the deep purple armchairs provides light and shade.

BELOW A splash of outrageous colour, seen here in the shape of a gloss-painted orange console, is a cheeky device to relax the formality of a room. Be experimental: choose a bargain piece of fleamarket furniture with a curvy silhouette, and paint it in a bright shade. **RIGHT** It's fun to jumble lots of bold colours together – great in a relaxed family space – but use white paintwork and pale timber surfaces to cool things down.

For some, a vibrant family home, bursting with colour, constitutes a casual interior. But tread carefully, as too many bright tones can be over-stimulating. An inspiring shade on just one wall, on glossy kitchen cabinets or on two or three pieces of furniture, such as a sofa or a console table, adds personality and whimsical appeal. By all means pick a shade you truly love, but choose one that will sit happily with neutrals, too – tangerine, amethyst or leaf green are softer on the eye than primaries. Introduce colour using the unexpected. Rather than employing cushions as a customary splash of colour, paint colour across the ceiling, or use it for giant drum lampshades so that it hangs tantalizingly in the middle of your space.

The key to using colour, whatever strength you choose, is not to stress about it. Casual living is just that – tapping into what feels right, and playing with the impromptu. Don't strive for perfectly matched colours and tones – experiment and see what works best. Forget about painting ten different sample shades on the wall – you will only confuse yourself. Just pick one and go for it. Often the most relaxed scheme is the one that grows in an organic way, as colour is added bit by bit.

OPPOSITE In a busy family kitchen, one wall has been painted with blackboard paint, for shopping lists and bird-watching. The black-painted pantry door doubles up as an impromptu pinboard. **BELOW** Subway-style white tiles always look crisp, but seek out variations on the theme. In this relaxed kitchen, more unusual Carrara marble versions look softer with the grey-painted units.

simple surfaces

We touch surfaces on a daily basis, so pick worksurfaces, floors and splashbacks that are deliciously tactile. Certain surfaces dominate large areas, and are a critical element in the design jigsaw, so think of them in terms of colour and finish, too. Do you like matt or glossy, subtly patinated or distressed textures? Surfaces should make your life run smoothly, so make easy-care choices.

ABOVE LEFT A painted pine tabletop is practical and offers myriad decorative possibilities. The peeling paint and timber can be mixed with utility china and plain glass tumblers, or teamed with a pretty lace runner and translucent porcelain for a casual yet sophisticated finish.

ABOVE RIGHT Consider using salvaged tiles in a bathroom, to elevate a plain and simple white sink into something a little more decorative and unusual. Often reclaimed tiles can only be found in restricted quantities, so they are perfect for creating a small area of splashback.

Casual living is all about making daily chores simple and quick, and that includes cleaning worktops, vacuuming floors and keeping furniture pristine. We all want good-looking surfaces, but make your choices with practicality in mind. If in doubt, ask questions when buying; the last thing you need in a kitchen are surfaces that stain easily. What are your priorities in terms of style? Do you want a slick surface that maintains its sparkling good looks, or a reclaimed material that looks better with every scratch?

Wood is warm, natural and, with a quick polish, comes up beautifully. It's brilliant for flooring, as it

ABOVE LEFT Exposed brickwork, painted in a deep shade, offers a dramatic blank canvas for an array of decorative kitchen accessories.

ABOVE RIGHT This 1960s home has solid oak floors throughout. When adding new wooden floors, look out for options such as a 'brushed' finish, which raises the grain, or buy reclaimed floorboards that already have a patina.

improves with age. Reclaimed floorboards come in a variety of choices, including extra-wide and parquet designs. Original floorboards can be sanded and waxed or painted with floor paint. New wood floors can be expensive: robust mid-priced alternatives are engineered boards that have a top hardwood veneer with core layers beneath. Wooden floors are easily vacuumed and need an occasional wash with detergent. Boards treated with Swedish lye soap look beautiful, but are high maintenance – you have been warned! Wooden worktops, whether new or reclaimed, need to be oiled occasionally.

BELOW LEFT A partially stripped surface can produce quirky decorative effects. Here, raw brick walls have been teamed in a tongue-in-cheek manner with a papier-mâché bear head by Emily Warren.

BELOW CENTRE If you're lucky enough to have original timber panelling, celebrate its wobbly simplicity. This portion of panelling is casually adorned with rakishly hung antique prints.

BELOW RIGHT White tongue and groove panelling is an instant way to smarten up a basic white bathroom suite. As it covers the walls, there is no need for tiles, so it's a simple and crisp surface to choose.

Exposed brick walls offer understated charm and are remarkably versatile. They fit perfectly in a country setting and also look edgy in a city apartment, painted white or in a deep shade. Too much brick can be overpowering – a single wall will create sufficient drama. For a truly dressed-down look, don't over-clean your masonry and leave the odd patch of plaster or flaking paint on view.

Plain painted walls are the ultimate fuss-free surface to live with, but it pays to experiment with paint finishes. Try gloss paint on your walls for a slick, wipe-clean city finish, or in a country house use a traditional limewash paint, which provides relaxed, uneven coats of flat, opaque colour. A small expanse of blackboard paint is fun in a family house.

With its connotations of simple, seaside living, tongue and groove panelling automatically sets a casual tone at home. It's brilliant in bathrooms, kitchens and bedrooms in particular; once painted it is virtually maintenance free, and is quickly wiped down. It's also a clever way to level out uneven walls, and looks crisp and neat. Panelling featuring scaled-up rectangles or squares offers a more grown-up but still clean-looking alternative; consider fitting built-in closets to match.

Although tiles are marvellously practical, navigate your way through the design choices to the simplest styles. For walls or splashbacks in a kitchen, bathroom or utility room, subway-style brick tiles look smart; white or black are classic choices, but a bright coloured variation in an urban home looks funky. A dark

grout looks edgy with pale tiles. Porcelain tiles, in giant squares, make a sensible option for a kitchen or bathroom floor. Tiny mosaic tiles do look wonderful, but are not the most practical choice as – particularly when used on a floor – there is a lot of grout that will discolour. Marble or Corian is an expensive yet chic and low-maintenance alternative to tiles. If your budget is tight, use just a tiny amount for a vanity worktop.

Stainless steel and glass are modern choices for get-up-and-go living. Stainless steel scratches, period. Accept that, grab a bottle of baby oil or a specialist cleaner and smudges will wipe off in a millisecond. Stainless steel is a chameleon-like surface that looks appropriate in an urban space but, teamed with salvaged wood, also looks workmanlike in a country casual-style kitchen. Glass is an equally useful surface. Use it in a traditional interior as glazing on internal doors or as sliding panels in an urban apartment; all it needs is a quick spray with glass cleaner to sparkle. It also makes a brilliant splashback and worksurface. Get a professional glass company to spray one side in a colour, but to avoid a green tinge, it's essential to use low-iron glass.

TOP LEFT Although stainless steel is often used for smart, easy-care worksurfaces, splashbacks and floors, look out for other robust details such as stainless-steel kitchen cabinet handles. Catering-style stainless steel trolleys and preparation tables are also practical for a utility-style kitchen. **TOP RIGHT** A stainless-steel worktop with integrated sink is easy to clean, as there are no joins.

Use glass in a pared-down, traditional interior as glazing on internal doors or as sliding panels in an urban apartment; all it needs is a quick spray with glass cleaner to sparkle.

THIS PAGE AND LEFT Toughened glass looks sleek in an urban setting, and is a particularly versatile medium in open-plan living spaces. In this city family house, fixed and sliding floor-to-ceiling sandblasted glass panels screen the kitchen from the dining room without impeding light flow. The paper sculpture is by Japanese artist Manami Hayasaki.

FAR LEFT In this city bedroom, sheer unlined linen curtains are simplicity itself, yet their full-length design gives the room glamour, too. Rather than being fitted to the deep bay windows, they are hung from a suspension wire running straight across the bay. **LEFT** Odd pieces of vintage fabric, made into one-off cushions, provide a hit of quirky pattern and unusual colour.

fuss-free fabrics

Fabrics add movement, softness and colour at home. Combine gently crumpled, smartly smooth and cosily dense textures, from light-diffusing sheers to luxurious yet practical upholstery. Hunt out textiles that look crisp on a daily basis, with minimum effort and maximum decorative impact. Apply that rule to every fabric, from the humblest towel to full-length curtains.

OPPOSITE For easy curtains, look out for crisp fabrics, such as denim or thick cotton, which are also soft to handle. Such fabrics don't always require lining if used for window treatments. In this guest room, denim curtains set a relaxed tone, as do the cotton waffle blankets. Specialist suppliers of organic bedding are a great source of embroidered or plain quilts in crinkly cottons. **RIGHT** Good-quality linens are suitable for both window treatments and upholstery, making it easy to create a cohesive scheme. Unlined linen blinds/shades create a neat, fresh window treatment. The painting is by Danish artist Jette Segnitz.

LEFT Gathered curtains in a plain cotton are an crisp, inexpensive choice in a casual bedroom, but there are subtle ways to add extra interest. Stitching a bobble trim or grosgrain ribbon along the leading edge looks very pretty. **RIGHT** These sheer, almost translucent silk curtains have been tied to the curtain rings with jute string, for a relaxed look.

We ask a lot from our furnishing fabrics – and in the casual home, there's even more pressure for textiles to be both good looking and high performance. When choosing fabrics, knowing what style of curtains or upholstery you want helps, but do some research as well. It's impossible to gauge drape, texture or indeed pattern from the tiny swatches that fabric companies usually supply, so visit department stores or fabric showrooms to view show lengths. What happens when you scrunch a fabric – does it look prettily rumpled, or just a creased mess? Is your chosen textile suitable for upholstery; will it lose its easy-going crumpled appeal if it's lined? Steer clear of fabrics that are dry clean only.

If you love a gently dishevelled look, natural texture and the promise of a truly easy-care fabric, then linen, cotton and linen union (usually a mix of linen and cotton) are obvious choices, though lighter-weight variations aren't suitable for upholstery. There are linens in every shade –

OPPOSITE BELOW A baggy white cotton slipcover is so versatile: it can be accessorized with different cushions and throws from season to season. This one has been imaginatively teamed up with a cushion made from a vintage Australian tea sack.

THIS PAGE A battered leather armchair requires little maintenance and automatically adds a casual air. Look for a chair with a pretty silhouette, like this one, and team it with a silk or tapestry seat cushion to add a dash of chilled-out glamour.

including natural tones – and every weight, and the beauty of linen is that it can be washed at 40ºC/104ºF and looks its best when slightly creased. If linen is used for slipcovers, have them made up slightly large, to allow for shrinkage. Depending on the look you're after, cottons are inexpensive and remarkably versatile, from translucent muslin – brilliant for window sheers – to denim, which is great for upholstery, and printed cotton. A linen union, in a plain colour, is a failsafe choice for upholstery – it will retain its neat and crisp good looks, and is washable and durable. Classic ticking is another reliable choice.

In a sophisticated city casual home, it may be more appropriate to choose fixed upholstery styles and fabric that looks pristine on a daily basis and that won't pill or rub over time. If you like a smooth finish, choose 100% wool in a plain colour, wool mix weaves in tiny patterns, tweed or brushed cotton. For a dense but smart texture, options include jumbo corduroy, chenille or cotton velvet. If upholstery is fixed, go for a reasonably dark shade so that there are few worries about stains, or choose a large pattern like damask or even tapestry – great in a country casual setting. Striped horsehair is expensive, but has a lustrous sheen and is incredibly hard wearing.

ABOVE For a funky mood, look out for 1960s and 1970s sofas in low-slung shapes with original leather upholstery. Bottle green or red are a quirky alternative to tan.

FAR LEFT AND LEFT Use cushions to vary the mood on leather upholstery. While velvet suggests a slick city mood, gingham or ticking cushions give a more rustic finish.

RIGHT AND FAR RIGHT Scour antiques markets for pieces of embroidered cotton or lace tablecloths. Antique textiles, already gently worn in, are brilliant allies in the casual home. In this country bathroom, a piece of embroidered voile has been casually fixed across the window for privacy. Scraps of old lace or silk can be stitched into scatter cushions. Have fun mixing one or two really ornate textiles with simple white cotton bed linen.

When choosing fabrics, knowing what style of curtains or upholstery you want helps, but do some research as well. It's impossible to gauge drape, texture or indeed pattern from the tiny swatches that fabric companies supply, so visit their showrooms to view show lengths.

It's hard to go wrong with leather upholstery, but new leather can look cheap. If you buy new, choose leather that has been distressed so that it doesn't look too pristine. Old leather sets the best tone; ideally, it will already be nicely softened, with a worn patina. It needs minimal maintenance: occasionally treat it with saddle soap and buff with a soft cloth. Vintage fabrics also have a place in the casual home. There is a reason why antique linen sheets and tablecloths endure: they are strong and made to last, becoming softer and more tactile with age. Use vintage sheets for curtains and blinds/shades, light upholstery (such as chair covers) or to cover headboards. Antique fabrics may come with the odd stain or hole, but that adds to the relaxed appeal.

Upholstery and window treatments stay put, but other fabrics – cushion covers, tablecloths, bed covers – are moved or used on a daily basis. As well as being washable, these must only require shaking out or plumping up to regain their good looks in a moment. Have some fun with texture for cushion covers – think of softly knitted ones, gently worn floral chintzes or felted wool that keeps its shape. Easy, fresh table linens include non-iron seersucker in jolly checks, oilcloths or table runners made from hand-loomed vintage hemp, which are intended to look rustic and crumpled. As for bed coverings, traditional feather eiderdowns or quilted bedcovers, either satin or in cotton matelasse, look relaxed but smart.

RIGHT In this playroom, a whimsical frame, made from the wire supports for a strawberry cloche, has been fitted with wooden pegs and adorned with artwork, for a simple and ever-changing display. **FAR RIGHT** Play around with lighting expectations. In this sparely styled bedroom, the classic Jieldé lamp, more frequently seen on a desk, provides a cool contrast to the pretty bedding.

atmospheric lighting

An imaginative lamp is a dynamic addition, contributing colour, texture and shape to forgotten corners, or defining a ceiling. Great lighting is also a practical tool, delivering illumination in all the right places. Think of your lighting choices as fun accessories in your design wardrobe; choose versatile styles that you can move from room to room.

We all know how great it is to see ourselves in a particularly flattering mirror; how it highlights our good points and minimizes our faults. Well-planned lighting performs a similar function. When you have good-looking light fittings delivering perfect illumination in all the right places, you don't have to think twice. Rooms look fantastic, the atmosphere feels right and you won't have to change seats to get to a decent reading lamp. But there is more to easy-maintenance lighting than installing overhead low-voltage ceiling lights everywhere. They do create

THIS PAGE Decorative side lights must look great by day, and create a pleasing ambience at night. Look out for unusual glass, ceramic or resin lamp bases in bright colours or decorative finishes. Granny-style frilled silk lampshades or drum shapes made up in retro fabrics are a fun way to introduce personality into an otherwise simply decorated room. The painting is a portrait of the owner's grandmother. **OPPOSITE BELOW** A row of low pendant lights creates instant atmosphere at night, and defines a dining table by day.

THIS PAGE When choosing a light, think not just of shape and scale but also materials and construction. Here, the intricate layers of a pendant shade add a dash of glamour.

a quality, even light, but think of them as just the background source. Lamps fulfil a decorative, practical and atmospheric function, so make them the star focus and get the mix right.

Giant pendant lights look good in both an urban and a country interior, and add focus and drama to a room. If you are having building work done, plan lighting so that there is one – or several – pendant lights above your dining table or kitchen island unit. Industrial-style enamelled pendants, 20th-century design classics such as the Le Klint designs or brightly coloured drum shades exude city chic, while a prismatic glass shade gives

LEFT In this chic sitting room, a confidently low-hung pendant light provides the intimate illumination normally supplied by side lights. Perfectly positioned to bisect the view into the next room, it's also a little playful, and so reduces the formality of the enfilade arrangement. **BELOW** Every pendant light will be silhouetted against an adjacent wall.

Think about that when choosing a style. An ornate shaped light will look quirky and bold against a plain, strong-hued wall. But in a casual kitchen such as this, in which one wall is crammed with a mix of paintings by the owner's artist friends, a very plain shade is the best choice. Furniture chains are a wonderful source of inexpensive shades and fixtures.

a simple, clean look in the country. Adjustable rise-and-fall pendant lamps are particularly casual for easy dinners. Grand pendant lamps can look self-conscious, so temper a sparkling chandelier or a metal candelabra with a beamed ceiling or distressed-looking furniture, to mix up the mood.

The whole point about casual living is that although the ambience is chilled out, all the essential services are in the right place. Forward planning is the secret. When you plop down on the sofa, there should be a side lamp within arm's reach, or when you want to hunker down with the laptop in the home office, a task light should be ready to hand. Think about the positioning of lamps. Review every room, and work out all potential activities and which light will do the best job. You can never have enough lamps, and these days there is no excuse – chain stores are packed

with inexpensive lights of every type, from metal to blown glass. Side lamps can go wherever you want them. As well as all the obvious spots, such as on bedside and sofa tables, think of placing them on an open shelf or on a console in the hall.

Whether you live in an open-plan space, which requires zoning for different activities, or simply like to have the freedom to move around furniture and lighting as desired, floor lamps are an invaluable tool. Forget the fuddy-duddy standard lamp, with its turned wood base and frumpy silk shade – today's floor lamps are funky and functional. There are classic 20th-century designs like the Castiglioni Arco light or the Bestlite BL3, which is height adjustable, or pick fun, modern lights that cast an efficient glow as well as making a design statement. If you're going to move floor lamps around, look for designs on castors or those that are light enough to move with ease.

Task lamps need to combine functionality with good looks. There are design classics that look fantastic whatever style your interior – such as the Anglepoise 1227 and the Modernist Jieldé desk lamp, which comes in amazing colours – but there are plenty of inexpensive chain-store styles, too. Look for task lights that angle quickly and easily. In a bedroom, wall-mounted task lamps are a good option. Before fixing to the wall or headboard, lie down to work out the best position for reading in bed.

Once you have efficient lighting in place, you can't beat the odd frivolous fixture to add atmosphere. Mini lights twisted around shelves crammed with china or an overmantel mirror will create unexpected twinkle and instant ambience.

ABOVE LEFT Many mid-20th century specialist dealers and websites offer a choice of vintage lighting. When buying second-hand lighting, first make sure that the light has been rewired for 21st-century use.

LEFT Think of occasional side lights as decorative accessories, and weave them in as part of a casually composed still life. Here, an American metal chest of drawers provides a rough contrast to a classic side light.

LEFT Half the fun of keeping everything on display is that all your best-loved things, from an heirloom silver sugar bowl to a hand-painted dish brought home from a trip to faraway lands, are easy to remember and therefore use. It makes setting the table more inventive if everything is see-at-a-glance. **BELOW** Reserve one shelf or section solely for small or delicate items.

storage & display

Filled with the clutter of everyday living and constantly in use, closets and shelves are the unsung heroes of our homes. Yet if we arrange these useful pieces of furniture sensibly, storage can also be beautiful and imaginative. Aim for a practical mix of storage options, and experiment with built-in choices, customized vintage cabinets and chain-store buys, so that there is literally a place for everything.

OPPOSITE If it's accessorized in the right way, an open-plan shelf unit can become a decorative item in its own right. This beautifully distressed example, conveniently placed next to the dining table, is lit at night by a trio of industrial-style angled lamps. Take time to arrange your plates and glasses efficiently and attractively. Here, items are loosely grouped into categories: glasses at the top, plates and decorative serving plates lower down and giant platters at the base. For practicality, keep a feather duster to hand, and give surfaces a quick dust every now and then.

ABOVE Vintage pine fruit crates make inexpensive storage and look great, particularly in a casual setting. In this family kitchen, these crates have been fitted with castors, and are useful for toys or storing newspapers that are to be recycled.
LEFT In a sitting room, an armoire or linen press, with cupboards below and glazed upper sections, is a decorative storage choice. Chicken wire is a rustic alternative to glass in a country setting. Consider painting the inside of the armoire in a contrast colour, or use a patterned wallpaper. The painting is by Danish artist Jette Segnitz.

It is perfectly possible to pursue casual living on a 24/7 basis, but it will help to have great storage in place at the start. Having sufficient cupboards and shelves isn't enough: they may create the illusion of a tidy house, but if too many possessions are stuffed inside and there is chaos within, no one feels relaxed. So begin by reviewing your existing storage. Does it work well? Are there areas in the house where clutter tends to build up? If so, target these first. Give storage a hierarchy so that it's easiest to get at the things you need on a daily basis.

If you prefer a streamlined look, custom-built fitted closets are the best option. As well as building closets in specific rooms, add additional storage, perhaps on a landing or in a hall, or fitted into odd alcoves around the house to hold frequently used items like spare bedding and luggage. Custom-built closets are expensive, but have the bonus of providing tailored storage. If buying standard items, look for modular systems that offer options you can customize, mixing and matching hanging sections and shelves of different heights and widths.

Freestanding storage ranges from painted, distressed wooden armoires for a country casual interior, to metal, MDF/fiberboard or coloured lacquer sideboards for a city home. The more thought you give now to the items to be housed, the easier it will be to find things without stress. Customize your storage inside to make it work hard – fit plastic drawers, double hanging rails, hooks, acrylic shoe cubbies and adjustable shelves.

Some people shy away from open shelving, feeling that they don't want the pressure of keeping it tidy. But if open shelves are ordered and there is a planned place for everything, they offer a wonderfully casual, see-at-a-glance way to live. Whether you go for an entire wall of open shelves in a kitchen or one freestanding bookshelf in the

RIGHT AND ABOVE LEFT A pared-down living room needs a designated area for items in use every day. Giant rattan, bamboo or wicker baskets are a good choice. The lithograph is by Michael Kvium. **ABOVE CENTRE AND RIGHT** Chunky knobs and hooks are a brilliant way to add extra storage options.

TOP AND ABOVE Casual storage means that possessions are in order yet close at hand. **RIGHT** Fit an empty stretch of wall with a couple of open shelves and a table, and it creates an instant extra storage zone. Use an array of wicker baskets, decorative pots or even a cake stand to keep your books and stationery in order.

living room, the secret is not to keep things in strict order. Ease of access is most important so that you can retrieve (or put away) plates or clothes without removing the entire pile. The same goes for magazines and books. Stack them high and don't worry about keeping them super-tidy. What matters is that they have a home and everyone knows where it is.

Shelving units come in sleek city casual options like solid wood and aluminium, or rusted steel, solid wood or painted MDF/fiberboard for a country casual option. Some have horizontal shelves; others feature a mix of horizontal and vertical dividers, to give a gently haphazard look while still keeping items organized. A grid system that provides cubbyholes offers easy access storage, as do units that offer a mix of shelves, drawers and pull-down cupboard fronts – particularly handy in a sitting room. Freestanding shelves can be used as room dividers in open-plan spaces, so ensure that they work from both sides. A series of shallow shelves, with a lip at the front, is a great design for holding books or periodicals.

Every casual home needs a selection of open-topped boxes, baskets or crates. These provide the option for a quick tidy up for

anything from shoes to DVDs. Who has time, after all, to replace each DVD into an alphabetically arranged box, or align shoes on a rack? Choose attractive options, from round baskets to smart leather boxes or wire baskets, or customize utility items: old fruit crates, fitted with castors, make an excellent choice. And don't overlook the power of looping or hanging up everyday articles. It makes them easy to get at and, if you choose attractive, chunky hooks, creates a good-looking display, too.

LEFT In a dressing room or child's bedroom, generous open shelves are a brilliant quick-tidy solution for folded knitwear, outdoor clothes or sports gear that is in almost daily use.

ABOVE If you have no space for a dressing room, designate one corner of the bedroom as a dressing zone. Hang a mirror, stack up your prettiest shoe boxes and add a stool or a chair.

flowers & firelight

It's the little details, from fresh flowers to the glow of firelight, that inject an instant, easy ambience into our everyday living spaces. Walls and furniture are fixed, but you can actively use the ephemeral quality of flowers, candles and firelight to bring a room alive.
They will also create a mood of constant change, to promote a dynamic, not static, casual way of life.

LEFT Candles are your secret weapon at home. Light one as dusk gathers and you have instant ambience. Look out for unusual candlesticks, from brass to china, in junk stores, polish up your grandmother's old silver ones or just use inexpensive tealight holders. Have fun choosing candles: play around with unexpected colours, or look out for striped or spotty versions. **ABOVE, LEFT TO RIGHT** The simplest flower arrangements are often the best, and certainly the most casual. Ring the changes. Gather lots of tiny vases and place just one stem in each, or jam several bunches of a single variety into a plain glass vase.

THIS PAGE An open fire will always be the focal point in a room, so lavish attention on creating an easy, vibrant display. Encourage the whole family to use the mantelpiece so that there is an ever-changing array. The portrait of the King of Thailand was painted by the nine-year-old nephew of Thai artist Attasit Pokpong.

Everyone wants to live in a space that feels alive, so consciously employ elements that will bring vitality and movement to a room. Flowers are an easy first step. They add vibrant colour and organic form to your home – a small detail with a powerful impact. Likewise, tap into the ambience that dancing firelight or candlelight can bring to an interior. Flowers and firelight are finishing touches, as important as accent colours or cushions, and they work well because they appeal to our senses – from the fragrance of newly cut flowers to the crackle of burning logs.

Get into the habit of buying flowers on a weekly basis – it needn't cost a fortune. If you have a garden or a window box, plant flowers to snip off: tulips, roses and hydrangeas are all pretty and simple. Learn to buy cost-effectively at a flower shop or stall. A generous bunch of foliage, such as scented eucalyptus or vibrant lime-green euphorbia, is just as beautiful as a vase full of flowers, and greenery looks wonderfully casual. Buy seasonally – choose daffodils when they are plentiful in spring; berries in autumn. If you select blooms with scale and shape in

LEFT Flowers and vases are an easy short cut for bringing accent colour into a room. In this city sitting room, the vivid green used for scatter cushions is reinforced with a plain vase to match.

ABOVE Every working fireplace needs a log holder. Properly made baskets in wicker or rattan are sturdy, and if you hunt out a specialist maker, you'll be supporting your local crafts industry, too.

mind – sculptural alliums are great in a modern interior; full-blown peonies for a country home – just two or three are enough to fill the space. A bunch of identical flowers looks more casual than mixed arrangements.

If it's easy to arrange flowers in minutes, you're more likely to buy on a regular basis. Sort out your vases, house them somewhere that is easily accessible and have a selection of containers. A basic selection of glass vases should include a short cube and a tall cylindrical one for starters, as well as wide-mouthed styles and multiple small vases, for lining up on a table. Add plain ceramic containers in a few different colours, galvanized metal, vintage glass jars or bottles, or a slightly chipped porcelain or plain earthenware jug.

ABOVE LEFT If you buy a bunch of mixed flowers and foliage, separate out the contents and dot them around the house. Just one or two stems displayed in a bottle or jar have their own simple charm. Choose foliage or berries that offer an attractive silhouette.
ABOVE RIGHT If you have a special place at home for yoga practice or quiet contemplation, add a candle there, too. Light it, and enjoy just a few moments' peace.

If you have the luxury of a real fire, make time to rake it and lay it, and have logs or coal close by in an attractive basket. If a real fire isn't an option, today's sophisticated gas fires are realistic, or consider a wood-burning or multi-fuel stove, which come in a range of traditional or modern styles. For a particularly relaxed effect, pile up logs by the side of the stove. If firelight isn't possible, candlelight is the next best thing. Have a drawer full of candles that includes tealights, which are cheap as can be and can be lit every night, creamy pillar candles, textured beeswax and slender dinner candles. Invest in a quality, scented candle, too. Try fig in spring and orange or cedar in winter. Make lighting candles part of your routine, and your home will always feel alive.

casual rooms

We live in an active world, with space at a premium, so every room in your home must earn its keep. Focus on the function, space planning and key furniture early on, and your rooms will let you kick back and relax. Aim for interiors that exude magnetic charm; spaces you'll want to return to night after night.

On the chalkboard:

Floor Polish
CIF CREAM
BLEACH
CILLIT BANG (orange lid)

relaxed kitchens

Sparkling surfaces, streamlined cabinets and high-performance appliances are the building blocks of an efficient kitchen, but for a casual twist, you'll need to inject character, too.

A burst of punchy colour, a painting or two and a table and chairs for impromptu gatherings are also vital ingredients.

THIS PAGE In a busy family dining area, add several giant platters or bowls for fruit; it creates an eye-catching display. Group cookbooks where they're needed – in the heart of the kitchen. **OPPOSITE** Stainless steel and pure white have been used to create a crisp kitchen that's both workmanlike and chic. Items used on a daily basis are neatly arranged on the worksurface.

The kitchen is inevitably the busiest room at home, whether you live alone or as a family, so plan for that. For a room to work hard – and therefore effortlessly – it must be minutely detailed, but with nothing extraneous. Think for a moment of the casual simplicity of a holiday rental. The essentials are to hand and there is enough of everything, but the closets aren't stuffed to overflowing and surfaces are uncluttered. Aim for a similar mood in your own kitchen. The difference at home is that you can add little luxuries and personal touches on top of everyday essentials. Consider your kitchen as a casually styled living room, not just a spotless zone for cooking and eating.

LEFT In an open-plan kitchen and dining zone, use surface and colour as a link. The olive of the kitchen splashback is repeated in an array of vintage fabric cushions; the glossy white of the units echoed in the retro dining table and chairs.

THIS PAGE This budget kitchen has been customized with a quality iroko worksurface (added by a carpenter) teamed with a solid oak floor. Bright wall paint or a colourful tiled or glass splashback adds to a customized look. **OPPOSITE ABOVE LEFT AND RIGHT** A collection of 1960s and '70s china injects personality.

BELOW Casual living is all about confounding design expectations. The combination of old store cabinets and high-gloss ... been given a streamlined finish with a custom-made ... worksurface.

everything is to hand. In a large kitchen, an L-shaped or a U-shaped arrangement works well, or if you choose a long galley-style counter, team this with a large island unit, otherwise you will walk miles! Ensure that there is at least a 1.2m/4ft triangle, which allows you to travel in a triangle between the three key activities of food preparation, cooking and washing dishes unimpeded by ...

Size shouldn't matter so long as you plan carefully. The smaller the space, the more likely you are to create a relaxed but efficient work zone. In a tiny kitchen, combine ... a mix of open shelves and cabinets, teamed with an island unit to hold the majority of appliances. If there are high ceilings, take ... slimline cabinets right up to the ceiling and keep worksurfaces ... work, a compact kitchen will certainly feel bigger if it's knocked through into an adjacent room – ... footprint of the work zone itself remains small.

We may all dream of ... kitchen, but it's important to zone areas so that ...

OPPOSITE In this city apartment, the kitchen, dining area and sitting room are open plan. Kitchen appliances and units in varied shapes and materials, from weathered wood to stainless steel, promote a casual mood, and blur the boundaries between different zones. **ABOVE** Blend the style of your kitchen with other features. Here, vintage glazed cabinets echo the glass doors.

LEFT In a country kitchen, where appliances are freestanding, small occasional tables can be pressed into service to hold extras like cooking implements. However casual and relaxed your lifestyle, a giant kitchen clock is essential.

ABOVE Designate plenty of accessible, open-plan storage for everyday essentials. This selection of well-worn chopping boards is stacked and all ready for use, yet the boards are stored neatly on an old timber shelf unit on wheels.

human traffic. If you have planned a large kitchen/dining room, make provision for cutlery/flatware and china storage near to the table: a painted dresser, open shelves or a vintage glass-fronted display cabinet are all great choices.

Whether you opt for a sleek fitted kitchen or a more relaxed mix of furniture and unfitted cabinets depends on the style you prefer. Either works well in the casual home, and can be tailored to city or country living. What matters is that your kitchen has both personality and efficiency. By all means plan a bank of

pristine units – the perfect way to provide ample storage, while looking serene and sorted – but shake up the mood a little. Touches of creativity will help your kitchen feel more casual. For example, team lacquered acid-yellow cabinets with an exposed brick wall, create a splashback of brightly coloured subway-style tiles in between bright white cabinets or add a curvy freestanding retro-style refrigerator as a deliberate contrast to the straight lines of fitted units. If you wrong-foot style expectations, your kitchen instantly gains personality.

THIS PAGE Easy-care surfaces are essential in a country kitchen. A wooden block, salvaged from a butcher's, is used as a giant chopping board, and the antique table already has a gently worn patina.

An unfitted kitchen is trickier to plan as, rather than going to a specialist kitchen supplier for everything, it's down to you to mix and match cabinets, open shelves and appliances. Focus on your work triangle – once you know where the kitchen sink and key appliances will go, plan your storage around them. For a deconstructed look, architectural salvage yards are the place to start. Armed with your measurements, start off by picking vintage furniture, from an Edwardian painted dresser to metal factory shelves. Team

OPPOSITE Open shelves provide a super-organized budget storage solution in a busy family space. This kitchen uses every spare inch of space, with extra foodstuffs tucked into plastic crates on the floor, and colanders stacked under a butcher's block.

ABOVE Add small open shelves close to the cooker so that everyday foodstuffs are within grabbing distance.
LEFT Transfer essentials, from salt to sugar, into jolly containers to make cooking fun. The painting is by artist Lise Eriksen.

these pieces with reclaimed surfaces, such as a slab of old marble from a baker's or a length of teak from a school laboratory. Enlist the help of a creative carpenter. He will be able to cut worksurfaces to size, or perhaps customize old storage units to fit the available wall space. For a fresh, cost-effective look, pick a flat-pack kitchen from a big retailer, then customize with unusual handles, a beautiful reclaimed worksurface and a chunky table or butcher's block instead of an island unit.

Ultimately, casual living is about carving out more leisure time for yourself, as your hard-working home allows you to speed through the daily grind of everyday tasks. So look closely at your appliances. It's a false economy to hang on to old-fashioned ones. Newer models are often multi-functional – such as a combination microwave oven with a steam-cooking option – as well as more eco-friendly. All UK appliances now bear a EU energy label, with energy-efficiency ratings. In the USA, yellow EnergyGuide labels advise on how much energy an appliance uses. Those who eat, study and relax in the kitchen should also read the small print on noise levels. Paying that little bit extra for the quietest possible dishwasher or washing machine (the manufacturer will list its decibel level) will pay dividends in terms of a more relaxed ambience.

OPPOSITE An island unit is a pivotal zone, so plan it with care. If it is sandwiched between a run of kitchen cabinets and the dining table, position the sink and the dishwasher right here. Make a feature of the island by adding decorative yet efficient pendant lights directly above.
RIGHT In a family kitchen, the table will be a multi-functional space used for meals as well as homework, crafts and socializing. A dresser or armoire situated close by can hold books, tableware and art materials.
BELOW RIGHT Build up a wardrobe of attractive table mats, tablecloths and decorative runners so that an everyday tabletop can, in seconds, be transformed for a dinner party.

It's a prerequisite in most kitchens to have a table and chairs – somewhere to eat, chat and work. Although island units are popular, a sturdy table is just as user-friendly and more flexible because it can be moved. Fit castors (with brakes) and it becomes even more mobile. Ideally, have a butcher's block or a small table for food prep and a separate dining table. An industrial-style metal trolley is great in a city chic kitchen.

If a table is to double up for kitchen tasks, get the biggest one you can accommodate. It's human nature to pile things onto available surfaces, and the last thing you want in a busy family kitchen is to have to move fruit bowls or homework every time you need to chop vegetables. Ensure that the tabletop is robust and easy to clean: stainless steel, scrubbed pine and marble (though it must be well sealed) are all tried and tested surfaces. In an unfitted kitchen, add an extra-small table close to the stove to hold cookery books, pans and cooking ingredients.

Look for a relaxed style of dining table that can be smartened up for supper parties. Play with contrasting styles to keep the mood upbeat. Plain cabinets take on a softer mood when teamed with a wonderfully worn timber table, or add a scarlet toughened glass and steel table to a gritty urban kitchen dominated by stainless steel worksurfaces. Choose between a tabletop that wipes down in seconds – glass, lacquer or laminate – or one that will wear beautifully with age, such as an

oak country style in a raw timber finish, a patinated brass top or a hand-painted finish. Match your table shape to the way you like to entertain. Round styles with a central pedestal leg are sociable and good in corner spaces, while long refectory styles suit big supper parties. Tables that can extend and trestle table styles provide flexible options for entertaining.

Hunt down kitchen chairs that are light, easy to care for, comfortable and good looking. Avoid fabric-covered styles in the kitchen, unless they have machine-washable loose covers. Brilliant city casual choices include polypropylene, moulded ply, brushed aluminium or wood veneer options. For a country casual

BELOW LEFT Mixing a few decorative accessories with a plain, pared-down modern kitchen will relax the whole room and make cooking fun.
RIGHT By contrast, a rough and ready wooden fruit bowl works well in a casual country kitchen, especially when teamed with a scrubbed pine tabletop.

The casual kitchen also needs a dash of soul. However streamlined and tidy you are, make the effort to introduce your favourite things; they will inject personality.

mood, add a mismatched collection of old wooden chairs in similar shapes, all painted the same colour for a more cohesive look, or choose classic silhouettes like ladderback or Windsor chairs. Traditional galvanized metal French-café chairs are failsafe options. For a truly laid-back style, brilliant both in the city and country, gather an eclectic mix of chairs, from mid-20th-century classics like the Eames DSR side chair to a plain bentwood chair. Everyone can pull up a favourite style. Stacking styles or folding canvas chairs are useful in small spaces, or for accommodating last-minute guests.

At the heart of casual living lies a clever mix of practicality and easy nonchalance. Cooking in the casual kitchen should be a breeze, with all the implements you need to hand and enough space to get started. Yet most of us fall into two distinct categories when it comes to kitchen organization. Some like empty worksurfaces and equipment neatly stored out of sight; others relish myriad pans and food jars on display. Which kitchen personality are you? If you prefer a tidier approach, make full use of the many extras available when buying kitchen units, from deep pan drawers to internal cutlery/flatware drawers; pull-out

THIS PAGE In this compact city kitchen, elegant linen Roman blinds/shades, framed black and white photographs and giant lamps suspended above the table are essential elements for transforming the dining zone for intimate kitchen suppers.

OPPOSITE In this converted fisherman's cottage, a well-planned kitchen makes the most of the space. Cheerful encaustic tiles delineate the kitchen floor; reclaimed boards the living area.
LEFT Use pendant task lights to illuminate surfaces, but scale them down in a small area.
BELOW A shallow shelving unit is a brilliant solution for holding decorative bits and bobs.

baskets to plate dividers. For those who like implements literally to hand, plan carefully so that equipment doesn't end up in a jumble. Wall-mount knives onto a magnetic strip, hang pans from S hooks and group utensils into a wide-necked container or suspend them from a rail.

Apply the same casual rules for the storage of crockery, glasses, cutlery/flatware and table linen. In a busy, working kitchen, everything from plates and glasses to knives and coffee cups will be in almost perpetual motion, moving from table to dishwasher to worksurface. Make life easy for yourself! Whether stored on open shelves or tucked away in a cabinet, daily tableware should be in an easily accessible place, neither too low nor too high, and the space should be kept uncluttered so the table can be laid, or the dishwasher unloaded, in seconds. By all means stack bowls and plates, or nest big platters one on top of the other, but ensure that everything is accessible without hassle. Make sure table linens are close to the table: look for a table style with integral drawers, or store in a dresser close by. Formal china, crystal glasses and small appliances that are rarely used can be placed on high shelves or in cupboards/closets.

BELOW It's tempting to fill every wall with cabinets, but add a bench or sofa so that there's space to relax. Here, the sofa is conveniently placed between a cosy radiator and the cookbooks.

RIGHT This unfinished masonry wall means there is no need for a splashback. Play with texture: the glossy timber work-surface contrasts with the raw brickwork.

OPPOSITE The beauty of bespoke units is that they can use every spare inch. In this kitchen extension, very tall, slim cabinets house the owners' collections of retro china, teamed with narrow drawers underneath. Add something whimsical to personalize a plain kitchen: these lampshades are made from upturned vintage hanging baskets.

The casual kitchen also needs a dash of soul. However streamlined and tidy you are, make the effort to introduce your favourite things; they will inject personality. Treat your kitchen as a living room and decorate it with whimsical possessions. A good starting point is to add a dramatic or over-scaled painting to enliven kitchen cabinets. Some people baulk at the thought of art in the kitchen, but provided you have an efficient extractor hood for ventilation, a painting won't suffer. Art doesn't have to be wall-hung: casually prop a picture on top of the extractor hood itself. As an alternative, group family photographs in similar frames on the wall, cram an open shelf with retro glassware or choose a huge kitchen clock – always the focus of attention on a busy morning. Add decorative items to the kitchen with a tongue-in-cheek air, and everyone will enjoy them.

cosy sitting rooms

Combine deep, slouchy furniture, a roaring fire and cocooning textiles to create a sitting room with pulling power; a space you'll be drawn to relax in. Focus on practical issues, from an easy-to-navigate room layout to great lighting, then play up the ambience using tactile fabrics and personal touches.

THIS PAGE A sofa becomes twice as inviting when layered with snug wool and faux fur throws. Colourful blankets add freshness to plain upholstery. **OPPOSITE** In a townhouse, the rear half of a knocked-through sitting room has been transformed into a family zone. Everything is deliberately low, from the leather ottoman to velvet floor cushions, to promote a chilled-out atmosphere.

BELOW Divide up your sitting room into zones so that everyone can grab a friendly corner. Here, an old leather chair has been tucked beside the fireplace. A display of papier-mâché animal heads by Emily Warren add a quirky touch.
RIGHT AND FAR RIGHT Make your sitting room personal by adding simple, easy displays of unusual objects. Here, there's a mix of everything from a papier-mâché model of the owner's mother to a contemporary painting by Kate Sherman.

Kitchen living is all very well, but nothing beats the appeal of a proper, designated sitting room, however tiny. In fact, a small sitting room can be a bonus, as it's easy to make the space feel warm and intimate. The days of a sitting room used only for 'best' are over; this is the room you should want to make a beeline for on weekday evenings, not to mention great chunks of every weekend. Ensure that the heating is up to scratch, and sort out draughts before doing anything else.

Every room at home must multi-task, so early on ask yourself how the space might be used – for TV, for socializing, for reading the papers or a mix of all those activities? In a family home, will the kids use this room? With judicious use of deep colours, washable fabrics and cosy furniture, it's perfectly possible to create a chilled-out yet smart sitting room that everyone can enjoy. Next, assess what the room has to offer architecturally. Is it a focal-point fireplace, a deep-set window crying out for alcove seating or French doors onto the garden? Architectural cues can often kick-start your plans for the layout or the look of a room.

THIS PAGE For a casual, rustic look in the sitting room, focus on well-worn, gently battered textures, ideal in a family space. Here, an old leather armchair, hand-crocheted blanket and a distressed painted-metal standard lamp create a cosy yet colourful combination.

THIS PAGE This townhouse boasts grand architecture, yet the sitting room treads a fine line between tailored chic and a welcoming mood. The secret lies in grown-up fabrics – velvet in jewel colours and distressed leather – mixed with low-slung but elegant furniture. The armchairs are from South America.

In an open-plan apartment, it's important to zone the sitting area so that it has an identity and ambience of its own. In a big space, sliding glass panels or panelled wooden doors create a physical barrier, or use a freestanding bookshelf, a large sofa placed facing into the sitting area or a decorative screen to create a division. Choose identical elements that will make the two areas feel cohesive, such as limestone or wood flooring throughout, or similar tones on the walls. Then actively use colour and texture to delineate a change from one space to another. One deep, moody-coloured wall in the sitting area, or the use of a vibrant rug or patterned textiles can all make the sitting zone feel womb-like and appealing. A long, thin sitting room, created by knocking two rooms into one, needs care to create a different mood in each 'half'. In a family space, line one end with bookshelves and add the TV, computer and floor cushions, while keeping the other end more formal.

Furnishing a sitting room is all about comfort, and, given the chance, most of us will head straight for the sofa. So make that your priority. Take a long, hard look at your existing sofa. Do you like it? Is it comfortable? If you have brought it from a previous home, do its proportions look right in your new sitting room? If you answer 'no' to any of these questions, have no qualms about swapping or selling it, and starting afresh. The best sofas allow one person to stretch out fully, two to curl up comfortably and three (four at a push) to sit and watch TV. If space is limited, consider two small sofas, placed parallel or at right angles to one another. Opt for a design that has strong comfort value – with

ABOVE RIGHT Adding tongue-in-cheek artwork is a sure-fire way to help a sitting room feel casual. Here, enlarged police mugshots of Jane Fonda and Frank Sinatra have been re-coloured by the artist Robert Young.

RIGHT Deliberately mixing and matching precious pieces with inexpensive fleamarket buys will also keep the mood relaxed. Here, a still life in oils by British artist Harry Holland is hung above a vintage metal table.

ABOVE While beanbags are practical in a family chill-out zone, they can also work well with tailored upholstery if you choose them in cowhide, leather, linen or faux suede. Get them refilled regularly, to avoid sagging.

RIGHT If you've inherited antique pieces, edit carefully, retain the things you love and sell the rest. Mix up styles: here, a contemporary lamp base with a drum shade is a contrast to the gilded frame of the painting.

a high back and supportive arms, squishy feather cushions and well-sprung upholstery. An L-shaped modular sofa is a good choice in a modern space; a high-backed Knole sofa or a buttoned Chesterfield perfect in a country casual sitting room.

Choose other upholstered furniture that is comparatively light and easy to move around, to allow for impromptu rearrangements in the sitting room. At the very least, have another armchair – preferably two – in a low-slung style, sufficiently deep for curling up. Classic 20th-century shapes include Jacobsen's Swan swivel chair and Saarinen's Womb

chair, or for a country casual look, choose a Victorian wing chair, a 1930s club armchair or a bergère chair with a wide upholstered seat. A leather or buttoned fabric footstool doubles as a coffee table, provides extra seating and can also be used as a footrest. A couple of low side chairs with no arms are also useful when guests drop by. If you're buying new furniture, spare a thought for the planet. The occasional inexpensive chain-store buy is fine, but don't forget that vintage or salvaged finds are often just as quirky and inexpensive, although they may cost more if they need to be reupholstered.

*Furnishing a sitting room
is all about comfort, and,
given the chance, most of us
will head straight for the sofa.
So make that your priority.*

THIS PAGE In this barn-style new build, twin
armchairs have been given a relaxed twist,
using neutral linen with a cheery red stripe.
Polished plaster walls and a slouchy leather
sofa also impart an air of informality.

We all deserve squishy cushions to sink into at the end of a long day. Every sofa needs a few, although not so many that you have to toss them on the floor before sitting down. Buy duck-feather cushions rather than cheaper polyester fillings, and in a variety of shapes. Team over-sized square cushions with rectangular shapes and tiny square ones (great as neck or lumbar support when relaxing) with a few long, cylindrical bolsters.

A couple of giant floor cushions or beanbags make great additional seating, especially in a family home. For practicality, choose washable cushion covers in cotton,

THIS PAGE This 1960s house has a pared-down style, with a mix of mid-20th-century and modern furniture, but it has been planned with comfort in mind. The sheepskin on the chair, a perfectly angled reading lamp and a thick rug all promote relaxation. The vintage sunburst mirror adds a cheeky touch.

velvet, linen or patchwork. Avoid any that are uncomfortable to lie on – decorative buttons, sequins and shells can be scratchy.

Although relaxation and ambience are the watchwords in the casual sitting room, efficiency matters, too. So plan to add a coffee table, several small side tables and perhaps a slim console or sideboard in your sitting room. Multi-functional furniture is a boon in a small room. A coffee table with an integral shelf for magazines, a nest of tables or a low, firm stool that functions as a table or a seat are all brilliant choices. It is possible to buy extremely cheap and well-designed side tables on the high street, in everything from wood veneer to tempered glass, but if you take the time to scout around junk stores, there are whimsical decorative tables to be found, from gilded metal to painted wood. If they are a little scratched, so much the better. Match the height of occasional tables to your sofa and armchairs, so that a side light, or a book, is easy to grasp.

Opinions are divided when it comes to a book-lined sitting room. While some claim that books look messy, others assert that they furnish a room and add character. If you're after a casual, carefree look at home, books do offer a wonderful way

ABOVE To achieve a cool, uncluttered look in the sitting room, choose plain walls and tuck equipment like a DVD player into a cabinet. Here, a retro sideboard fits the mood. On the wall hangs a 1960s scarf by Richard Allan. **LEFT AND RIGHT** Display cherished pieces on a sideboard or tabletop. This 1960s West German pottery is arranged in simple groups.

LEFT A low coffee table is a must, for keeping reading material in order, while a firm upholstered stool provides extra seating. Pick easy-care surfaces: solid wood, toughened glass, leather or stone tabletops all work well. The prints on the mantelpiece are by Alan Kitching, Edward Bawden and Mimi Roberts.
OPPOSITE In this sitting room, the bespoke bookshelves define the room. The books are arranged rakishly, to avoid a formal look. 'Secret' double doors, built into the shelves, lead into a media room. The portrait was a lucky auction find.

to inject colour, pattern and personality. It's a classic choice to fill fireplace alcoves with built-in bookshelves, but this can feel overpowering. As an alternative, devote an entire wall to bookshelves, but face your sofa and armchairs away from them, or put shelves on an adjacent wall. Have fun arranging your books, but don't make them too regimented. Books look best if they neatly fill the shelf space, without big gaps at the top, so choose adjustable shelving and group similar-sized books together. Mixing alternate sections of vertical and horizontally

stacked books looks nonchalant. And remember, casual living is all about having things to hand. Take time to group books by subject or author so that it's easy to find your favourites.

A fireplace offers the most natural, and decorative, focal point in a sitting room. Of course, choose a style that suits the architectural mood of your home, but pick the simplest version you can find. Eschew fussy, carved marble or wood surrounds and patterned tile or cast-iron inserts, and go understated. In a modern sitting room, either a hole-in-the-wall style or an open

brick hearth with no surround looks crisp, and throws full attention onto flickering flames. Hang an over-sized painting or mirror above, to strengthen the point of focus. In a country casual sitting room, a surround in timber, stone or painted wood is appropriate, but look for very simple, linear styles with minimal decoration. A wood-burning stove is a cosy-looking alternative. A freestanding fire basket, teamed with a plain slate or limestone hearth, is a particularly casual look. Use your mantelpiece as a vehicle for an ever-changing display of things you love, invitations, photos and candles.

To feel truly casual, flooring must be tactile and warm enough to lie on. For many of us, hard flooring is still the preferred choice. If you are laying a limestone floor, underfloor heating is a must in a sitting area. And although a timber floor looks wonderful, even that can feel chilly. The answer is a large, textural rug: a colourful, abstract-patterned 100% wool rug or a funky shagpile design are both excellent choices in a city casual home, while in a country sitting room, experiment with a faded Aubusson, a kilim or a Portuguese needlepoint rug. Vintage rugs impart a wonderful, worn mood; who cares if they are a little

ABOVE AND RIGHT Bookshelves don't have to be built in. In this funky city sitting room, the owner has used a freestanding metal shelf, salvaged from an office and painted black. The unexpected mix of books, magazines, handbags and even shoes provides a flash of glamour.
OPPOSITE LEFT Every sitting room needs a comfortable chair for reading. This Marco Zanuso style looks laid back, and its pale upholstery is also deeply feminine.
OPPOSITE RIGHT In an open-plan space, use a piece of furniture to link different zones. This curvy Cherner chair does the trick.

faded? Fitted natural-fibre flooring such as coir or sisal has a relaxed, uneven texture, but can be rough underfoot. Either lay a rug on top, or choose a sisal and wool mix for the softest option. For ultimate comfort, go for a 100% wool fitted carpet in a neutral colour. These days, there are innovative, chunky weaves that have the look of natural fibres but the warmth of wool.

The sitting room performs a dual function: although it's a place where you want to feel cocooned and chilled out, it's also a 'public' room, a place to entertain friends and somewhere

to display your most treasured possessions or furniture. Make it your express aim to blend the two functions and create one cohesive, welcoming space. For example, if you have a grand painting, perhaps with a gilded frame, prop it on the mantelpiece rather than hanging it, or deliberately juxtapose it with a kitsch fleamarket 1950s vase, just for fun. An antique mahogany console table can be mixed with a contemporary side light, perhaps topped with a tangerine silk drum shade, to detract from its formality. Take an afternoon and experiment

BELOW AND RIGHT The casual home is an ever-evolving visual feast. Clever cushion choices will help. Pick one or two accent shades, teamed with a neutral, and make up cushions with contrast backs or multicoloured panels to ring the changes.

A fireplace offers the most natural focal point in a sitting room. Of course, choose a style that suits the architectural mood of your home, but pick the simplest version you can find.

with all your decorative accessories, playing around with different variations until you hit upon the right casual mix. And even then, make a mental note to swap things around every three months or so, to keep the look fun and fresh.

Once you have achieved a balance of formality and function in your sitting room, concentrate on the tactile, cocooning factor. Add a pile of blankets and throws, perfect for hunkering down in front of the television. They will look great folded over the side of an armchair, tucked right over an old sofa or piled onto a stool. If you have a neutral scheme, just one throw in a vibrant jewel shade will add a welcome note of accent colour.

A cashmere throw is expensive and therefore an investment, but is the ultimate treat – choose a dark neutral colourway that won't require too much washing, or a striped cashmere blanket. Other wonderful alternatives are Scottish Aran knitted throws, checked Irish mohair, which often comes in vibrant hues, Peruvian alpaca throws, which are very light and soft, or mohair or lambswool throws in plain, deep shades. Vintage Welsh blankets or old picnic rugs are particularly appropriate in a casual country sitting room. A sheepskin is another cosy and tactile alternative. Toss it over a chair back or onto a low stool for an extra hit of warmth.

THIS PAGE A modern, pared-down sitting room can still feel intimate, but pay attention to the key elements that will add mood. In this townhouse, the owner has used a painting of an Irish landscape by Hugues Pissarro dit Pomié as a focal point, as it's a reminder of her native Ireland. Everything in the room links back to the painting, from the dark leather upholstery to the wood-burning stove, and the flashes of vibrant green on the silk cushions.

**THIS PAGE AND OPPOSITE
RIGHT** If you're planning a
sitting room, and already
have an array of furniture
in many different styles,
it's helpful to find one or
two pieces that can act as
strong decorative anchors.
In this family sitting room,
a pair of armchairs is
upholstered in hot pink.
Neutral walls and flooring
give them emphasis, and
as one chair is placed at
each end of the room,
they work hard to pull
everything else together.
The naïve-style painting
was bought in Thailand.

ABOVE In a sitting room with white walls and an eclectic mix of furniture, there is the perfect excuse to amass an unexpected collection of treasured possessions. Here, brightly coloured oddities, from toy cars to mini Buddhas, look fun and quirky.

THIS PAGE Keep your bedside table uncluttered. The items you store on it are the first things you'll see every morning, so make them beautiful. In this elegant, simple room, a glass-topped table and clear glass lamp base exude purity and calm. Restrict cosmetics to essentials only, and add a bowl to hold jewellery, loose change and your phone.

OPPOSITE An upholstered bedhead is a cosy luxury. French antique styles look fresh when buttoned in a plain fabric. A satin eiderdown adds a dash of frivolity. The portrait of a woman propped against the wall is by British artist Ruskin Spear.

tranquil bedrooms

For a chilled-out bedroom, focus on curvaceous lines, muted hues and an inviting bed. Plan multi-tasking window treatments to allow for precision light control and add cushioning surfaces, from soft rugs to tactile bedding, to promote relaxation.

As the place where we start and end each day, the bedroom has a particular responsibility. It should help us feel calm, yet must be well organized so that we can find everything in the morning. It is the most private room in the home, a sanctuary and a place for rest, but it can also be an energizing space. It's a busy world out there, so if you want to pursue a casual lifestyle, with as much relaxation time as possible, the organization starts here. Casual living is all about finding a happy medium at home: a balance between order, comfort and chilled-out style. Make sure your bedroom incorporates all three.

The bed is the focal point and the biggest object in the room, so make it work hard for you. A good night's sleep is integral to feeling relaxed, therefore comfort is a priority. A pocket-sprung mattress is the quality option, or if not, choose open coil springs. A Tempur mattress, made from temperature-sensitive material that yields slowly

ABOVE Choose cocooning textiles in the bedroom. In this barn-style new build with floor-to-ceiling windows, quilted curtains keep out chills and pool luxuriously on the floor. **FAR LEFT** Your bedroom is a private place, for relaxing or thinking. Add an armchair or chaise longue, but don't clutter it with cast-off clothing. You can get away with more delicate pieces in the bedroom: this armchair is very worn, but has a threadbare beauty. **LEFT** Muted shades make for a soothing room, but one or two gorgeously patterned cushions add colour and life. **OPPOSITE** To show off the wonderful patina of the antique four-poster, the rest of this bedroom has been kept monastically plain, with pale painted walls and floorboards.

THIS PAGE A moody, dark scheme can be very tranquil. As this city bedroom benefits from floor-to-ceiling windows and a leafy view, dark grey blinds/shades, upholstery and a dark floor create an ambient contrast.

under pressure, is expensive, but forms to your body shape. For extra softness, there is an array of mattress toppers that vary from goosedown to latex – a good choice for allergy sufferers.

Take time to review your bedding. If you're making the bed and whizzing out of the door, you'll want pillows and a duvet/comforter that plump up in seconds. Goosedown pillows are the luxury option, but for firm support, go for a Tempur pillow. Choose a duvet/comforter that shakes out easily: a boxed construction will keep the filling evenly distributed. Visit a showroom and feel the weight and texture of different duvets/comforters. A goosedown filling will be the lightest and softest, and is practical, as it can be washed. But for a hypoallergenic choice, a silk-filled duvet/comforter is a more unusual option. Silk can't be machine-washed, but is easily aired outdoors.

Of course, the look of the bed is important, but comfort matters, too. So if you're buying a new bed, try out different styles in the showroom. Your choices are a simple divan/box spring, with or without a headboard, or a decorative bed frame. A padded headboard is easy to team with a divan/box spring

ABOVE If you are a keen reader, fit angled reading lights to the wall above the bed, leaving room on the bedside table for piles of books.

LEFT Blankets and throws are cosy extras. In a sober monochrome scheme, use texture to ring the changes, from self-stripes to herringbone weaves.

RIGHT Vintage metal chests of drawers provide a more relaxed look than traditional wood versions.

ABOVE Look for an interesting alternative to the ubiquitous wicker laundry bin. This vintage utility style becomes a quirky piece of furniture in its own right. **LEFT** Add tactile materials. In this mellow bedroom, thick curtains and a soft quilt provide an intimate atmosphere. The painting is by Russian artist Irina Rudneva. **OPPOSITE ABOVE LEFT** Dress a bedroom mantelpiece with a light touch. A photo or two, tucked into a mirror, are all you need.

base (choose one with drawers for extra storage). For a clean, simple look, choose a plain style with a removable slipcover in linen or cotton (preferably one that is machine-washable), or go for a buttoned headboard in a dark-coloured, tactile fabric such as chenille or brushed cotton. A restrained four-poster, in wood or metal, looks wonderfully casual with sheer linen or voile curtains tied along the top. Team an antique bed in a classic style – a French Louis-style caned headboard, or a brass bedstead – with crumpled linen to avoid too formal a look.

The bed is the focal point in a bedroom, so pay attention to how it's dressed. In the casual home, there are two choices: either go for easy-care bedding that needs minimal ironing or choose bedding that looks fabulous when gently creased. There is no shame in choosing a poly/cotton mix, as the bed linen looks crisp, won't need ironing and is inexpensive. Alternatively, look out for textural seersucker or soft cotton piqué, or choose sateen cotton bed sets, which are quick to iron. Avoid styles with pintucks and complex drawn thread work, as they can prove a

the ultimate choice is 100% linen: either buy new

casual bedroom. For a cheaper but still good

no one wants to remove endless scatter cushions

ABOVE CENTRE A traditional feather-filled eiderdown is a fantastically glamorous, yet easy, way to dress a bed. A specialist company will re-cover a second-hand eiderdown for you. **ABOVE RIGHT** If you're after a simple but romantic mood, choose curvaceous accessories. In this country master bedroom, a lamp with the prettiest pleated silk shade adds elegance. **RIGHT** Furniture needs to double up when space is tight. This gently worn table works as both a bedside table and an impromptu dressing table.

BELOW An all-white bedroom is soothing, but pick one or two key elements to soften the look. In this room, crushed raspberry cotton pillow slips and a cheery flower-embroidered waffle blanket add the right amount of colour.

RIGHT If there's no room for a dressing table, the top of a chest of drawers will suffice. Don't over-clutter: hang jewellery from wall hooks nearby, and keep only everyday cosmetics to hand. Store everything else in the bathroom.

before climbing into bed. Pick a throw, bedcover or quilt that is easy to care for – check the washing instructions and avoid items that are dry clean only – and that looks just as pretty gently rumpled as smoothed flat. Great options include crinkly voile or quilted cotton quilts; pick a sorbet shade like raspberry or ice blue, or a dark tone such as aubergine or chocolate. For a plainer look, add a cable-knit wool throw, a cotton waffle blanket or a shearling throw folded at the end of the bed. Extra blankets and big square pillows for lazy Sundays can be stored in a blanket box at the end of the bed.

One of the secrets to casual living is that if the home surroundings are kept simple, a chilled-out existence automatically follows. Remember that, and make sure every piece of furniture has a function, as well as looking great. The more streamlined your bedroom, the more tranquil it will be. Good bedside tables are essential. Pick a style that has at least one drawer, that sits level with the bed and that has sufficient room for a lamp, phone, clock and books. In a slick urban

THIS PAGE In a small room, it's vital to create an illusion of order and space. Here, built-in flush closets have been sunk into both chimneybreast alcoves, so are virtually invisible, and under the high bed, baskets store spare bedding. What do you see when you lie in bed? Pick a beautiful painting: this one is a treasured junk-store find.

LEFT Because the bedroom should be atmospheric and tranquil, combine a mix of lighting options, and always fit dimmer switches. Here, in place of a conventional bedside light, the owner has corner-hung a chandelier for sparkly low-level illumination. Dark grey walls create a subtle but atmospheric backdrop for mood lighting. **OPPOSITE** In place of a chest of drawers, experiment with quirky alternatives that will become a focal point. This bedroom boasts an original shirt cabinet, salvaged from a gentlemen's outfitters. The glazed compartments provide handy see-at-a-glance storage for everyday garments.

apartment, a high-gloss lacquered table in a bright colour or a dark wood like walnut will look cool. In a coastal or country-style home, a painted table or a vintage metal locker are easy choices. For a mix and match look, choose two different tables, or paint contrasting styles the same colour for a loosely matched look.

When planning clothes storage, think about daily clothes management. Casual living is about having your things in the right place, not about casting possessions on the floor. If you

know you won't diligently hang up your clothes every night, plan for that: have a chair or ottoman ready to take discarded garments, or, in a feminine bedroom, a tailor's dummy can be a quick way to hang up clothes. In a stripped-back urban bedroom, wall-mount metal hooks for jeans and jackets, or add a delicate hook in a country casual bedroom, complete with a padded hanger. An open-topped sisal basket tucked behind an armchair is great for a quick tidy-up of shoes and exercise kit.

If the bedroom is to feel tranquil yet casual, there must be adequate clothes storage, not to mention space for shoes, bags, luggage, cosmetics and jewellery. If you are blessed with enough space to create a walk-in closet, or indeed an entirely separate dressing room, plan it minutely so that everything is easily accessible. A mix of double-height and single hanging rails, deep shelves for jeans and jumpers, shallow drawers for underwear and socks, and racks for shoes will help with organization. Small details really do make a difference, from having proper padded, wooden and skirt/trouser hangers so that items are easy to put away, to storing out-of-season clothes in zip-up bags on a top shelf. The better organized your clothes, the simpler getting dressed becomes.

If clothes are to be stored in the bedroom itself, built-in closets, either in alcoves or built across an entire wall, offer seamless storage without cluttering the room. But if you do choose freestanding storage, pick a style that won't overpower; there is nothing very tranquil about lying in bed looking at huge armoires. In a city casual bedroom, vintage metal lockers, glass-fronted salvaged display cabinets or the sleek lines of a 1960s teak wardrobe will all look cool and unfussy. For a country bedroom, a mirrored or Gustavian-style painted armoire are pretty choices. Choose styles that aren't too tall so they don't feel crammed into the space, and look for options that feature glass or mirror detailing, or pale paint finishes and bleached wood, which will feel less overpowering.

Even if you have a walk-in closet, it's desirable to have a chest of drawers (or two) in the bedroom. Gravitate towards styles with a slim silhouette – 1960s and '70s furniture often looks very sleek, for example – and with pretty legs, from cabriole legs on an antique style to slim metal legs on modern pieces. Look for attractive surfaces, too, so that the chest of drawers becomes an appealing piece in its own right, rather than just a block of functional storage. Mirrored or metal-leafed

When choosing storage, think about daily clothes management. If you know you won't diligently hang up your clothes every night, plan for that: have a chair or ottoman ready to take discarded garments, or, in a feminine bedroom, a tailor's dummy can be a quick way to hang up clothes.

styles are glamorous in a city casual bedroom, while a painted finish or a marble-topped version is great in the country. A dressing table is the perfect place to create a casual display of treasured things. Loop beads over a mirror, jumble bracelets and earrings into bowls and show off pretty perfume bottles.

With the basics sorted, create ambience in the bedroom – it doesn't just happen. Get the lighting right. Window treatments should keep out light when you are sleeping, so either line or interline curtains or use black-out blinds/shades. Plantation shutters, unlined blinds/shades and semi-translucent sheers are atmospheric, as they filter sunlight prettily. Overhead lighting should be bright enough to allow you to get dressed, but fit a dimmer switch for ambient lighting. Even if you have low-voltage ceiling lights, it's an attractive option to team them with a statement pendant light, whether a metal chandelier in a country bedroom or a retro glass shade for city casual chic.

Don't forget the little extras. Add paintings, prints or framed photos of your favourite people. Casual living is about being relaxed in your own space – so own it.

ABOVE In this top-floor bedroom, picture windows overlook trees and sky, so there's no need for window treatments. For light sleepers, fit black-out roller blinds/shades. In a room with a view, keep the interior simple. Here, a retro chest of drawers and stool are understated. The picture is a framed vintage fabric panel. **RIGHT** Keep a pair of binoculars close by for enjoying the view.

THIS PAGE If the bed is a plain divan/box spring with no headboard, use decorative cushions to provide a focal point. Vintage silk squares, backed with cotton, can be stitched into eye-catching, easy cushions. **OPPOSITE BELOW RIGHT** Display decorative bangles in bowls, and store the rest to avoid over-cluttering.

THIS PAGE In a busy household, twin sinks can be a boon. Look out for unusual double designs like this at salvage specialists. The joy of casual living is that key items don't have to match. These auction-bought mirrors are similar, but not identical.

THIS PAGE If space permits, situate the tub in the middle of the room, so as to maximize a great view from the window. A pure white scheme is always tranquil, but the gentle veining on the marble adds warmth. Pick bathroom fittings with smooth, clean silhouettes for easy cleaning and a crisp finish.

soothing bathrooms

Pristine, sleek surfaces and clever space planning are essential factors for a casual, simple bathroom. But although white fittings and fluid contours will promote a relaxing, easy-living mood, don't be afraid of colour. Use it for tiles, flooring or accessories to shape, personalize and bring vigour to a bathroom.

THIS PAGE To create a particularly relaxed mood in the bathroom, pick organically shaped fittings, such as this luxurious egg-shaped bath. Keep other elements fluid to maintain a casual ambience. In this bathroom, towels are simply folded over a painted ladder, propped against the wall. A giant rug takes the place of a conventional bath mat.

LEFT AND FAR LEFT Bathroom accessories should be hard-working yet also pleasing. Choose a tiny hand-painted dish as an alternative to a soap holder, and stash spare toilet paper in a canvas or strong paper sack, such as this whimsical design. **BELOW** Introduce decorative elements to the bathroom to personalize the space. Here, an unusual cabinet and a carved wooden door add texture and pattern.

A bathroom has to deliver on several fronts. As well as being a place to relax on weekends and evenings, it must also be a pared-down yet no-fuss space where getting washed and ready for the day can take place with minimal fuss. Whether you are planning a bathroom from scratch or upgrading an existing one, focus on the plumbing, heating and ventilation first. Excellent water pressure makes all the difference, and adding a booster pump can improve it dramatically. A warm bathroom is a relaxing bathroom. Ideally, combine a radiator with a heated towel rail/bar – and underfloor heating is a great luxury. Pick a towel rail/bar with widely spaced bars so that it's easy to replace towels in seconds. Make sure the windows open easily, to let in a summertime breeze, and position the tub to have a great view of the sky.

Don't just pick a bathtub because it looks great: consider comfort, too. Get into the tub in the showroom and check out its slope, length and width. Decisions will include whether you want the bathtub to be freestanding, if you want central pillar or wall-mounted taps/faucets and whether you are after a modern or traditional style? A roll-top tub is an enduring and comfortable classic.

Teamed with ball and claw feet, Victorian-style taps/faucets and a pastel-painted exterior, it looks great in a rustic bathroom. Left with a raw metal finish and plain feet, it's dramatic for an urban look. Expensive but beautiful variations include boat and slipper bathtubs, which come with wonderful exterior choices, from a polished and lacquered iron finish to a patinated copper one.

For a neat, pared-down look, pick a plain steel bathtub, designed to be built in or fitted behind a panel – painted tongue and groove, tiles and glass are all smart easy-care panel options. In a modern bathroom, avoid trendy contemporary tubs, as they will date. Some of the prettiest around are freestanding ones with gently rounded contours. Modern tubs are often acrylic, so warm up quickly

ABOVE AND RIGHT In a busy family bathroom, surfaces must be easy-clean and robust. Here, a mosaic-tiled floor and wall are practical, and the square, boxy sinks and bath have a no-nonsense utility feel. Avoid a clinical look; in this bathroom, white is used as a background for bright accessories, from towels to tooth mugs.

and are a breeze to clean. When deciding where to position the tub, think ahead and work out where you will comfortably stash your bath products, a book or a drink. A built-in bathtub can have a narrow shelf running around it, or you can place a small pedestal table next to a freestanding tub.

If at all possible, invest in a separate shower enclosure rather than a shower over the bathtub. Keep it simple with your shower choices – it's not essential to have a vast choice of jet options. A decent width shower rose (20–25cm/5–8 inches), with a choice of firm or gentle water pressure, is all you need. All-glass shower cubicles are very popular, but spare a thought for the amount of cleaning they require. For the ultimate fuss-free shower, have a walk-in tiled shower zone, with no need for a door, or a single glass door. Team with white, black or brightly coloured subway tiles in a city bathroom, or French glazed ceramic tiles in a pretty colour like raspberry or leaf green for a country space. Large patterned encaustic tiles look stunning on the floor of a walk-in shower.

Think of your sink as a piece of furniture: it must be functional yet beautiful. Where are you going to put daily essentials, such as soap and your toothbrush? Either choose a version with

The key to creating a carefree bathroom is to ensure that it has a dash of personality. Play with your bathroom; think of it as a living room. What can you add, once the basics are in place, to make it a cheerful place to relax in?

RIGHT A bathroom should cater for quick bath times, or a luxurious soak, so pick accessories accordingly. In this country bathroom, a giant clock ensures that no time is wasted in the morning, but a side table holds bath products, candles and brushes. The casual bathroom is a breeze to clean, yet informal. Here, plain white tiles are practical, but the battered side table creates a relaxed, room-like feel.

a broad surround, an undermount sink sunk into a countertop, a vessel sink on a counter or a pedestal design with integral soap dishes. Attach a liquid soap dispenser and a tooth mug to the wall for an uncluttered mood. A sink featuring a towel rail/bar is space efficient in a small bathroom. Many pedestal or console-style models have them, or choose a traditional ceramic or marble-topped washstand/vanity with a towel rail/bar. Twin sinks are an asset in a family bathroom. Choose taps/ faucets in brass, nickel or chrome, with fuss-free,

ABOVE AND ABOVE RIGHT In a small bathroom, choose fittings that maximize space. This wall-mounted sink frees up the floor, and a bamboo towel rail/bar adds texture to a clean modern scheme.
RIGHT It's a nice touch to include a built-in bookshelf in a bathroom. Here, cabinets have also been sunk into the wall.

THIS PAGE In an elegant city home, it's still possible to have an easy-living bathroom. The sleek modern twin sink is super-efficient, but has been teamed with a classic roll-top tub, a decorative encaustic tile floor and an ornate mirror, to add glamour. The drawing is by Sarah Herman.

easy-clean styling. Wall-mounted versions with a mixer spout or classic lever styles are slick in a city bathroom, or pick pillar taps/faucets to match a classic pedestal design.

Efficient storage will keep your bathroom neat yet casually ordered. If you are installing a new bathroom, consider sinking a cabinet with a flush mirrored door into the wall, or adding a couple of alcoves above the tub or in the shower to hold

ABOVE With an over-bath shower, tiled or stone surfaces are essential. In this cottage, fresh blue and patterned tiles create a breezy, practical effect. Reconditioned fittings add personality to a bathroom, as does a vintage metal medicine cabinet.

toiletries. A storage cabinet can hold everything from toilet paper to cosmetics. In a city casual space, choose a funky option like a vintage polished metal apothecary cabinet. If you prefer a more casual arrangement, stash bottles and creams on a glass or metal trolley on castors. Fold spare towels onto luggage rack-style metal shelves, or hang them over a bamboo ladder, casually propped near the bathtub.

Time spent in the bathroom should be a soothing experience, so choose tactile accessories. If you prefer thick, fluffy towels, check out the gsm (grams per square metre) rating before buying – the higher the gsm, the greater its absorbency. Anything above 700 gsm is perfect. In the summer, exchange cotton-loop towels for waffle ones, which are light and absorbent, or try stripy, colourful Turkish hamman towels, hung from hooks close to the shower. Never wash standard towels using fabric conditioner, as it reduces their ability to fluff up. White towels are a classic choice, but they will grey over time. These days there is a wonderful choice of other colours, from jewel shades to subtle hues such as putty, charcoal or sage. Treat yourself to a good-quality cotton bath mat, or consider a washable cotton rug or a sheepskin to take the chill off a tiled floor.

The key to creating a carefree bathroom is to ensure that it has a dash of personality. Play with your bathroom; think of it as a living room. What can you add, once the basics are in place, to make it a cheerful place to relax in? If there is space, adding a single quirky piece of furniture works wonders, from a low armchair with a brightly coloured cotton loose cover to a full-length mirror with an ornate gilt frame, which will soften the effect of white bathroom fittings. Hang an oil painting that you love in direct view of the tub, or include a bookshelf. And treat yourself to luxury bath products – it really will make a difference. Fragrant organic bath oils, a quality scented candle or pastel-hued hand-milled soaps casually piled into a dish will all help to transform your bathroom into a chilled-out haven.

THIS PAGE If space allows in a downstairs toilet or utility room, add a wet-room shower. With its mosaic tiles, stone floor and giant showerhead, this one is no-nonsense and efficient. The walk-in design means there is no need for an enclosure. A vessel sink and wall-mounted taps/faucets free up space to house twin laundry bins.

THIS PAGE Choose robust materials for children's rooms – tongue and groove and painted walls are easy to touch up. The alphabet flashcards are by Lisa DeJohn.
OPPOSITE Kids love to have their own table. Look out for vintage school desks, which will already be gently scuffed.

children's spaces

See key family zones through a child's eyes, and planning will be easy. Kids' spaces are the places where quirky detail, gently distressed surfaces and enticing colour can collide. Get to grips with efficient storage, and plenty of it, so that you have the perfect balance of order and originality.

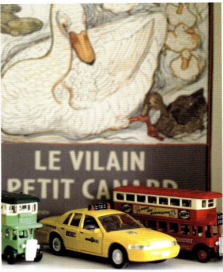

ABOVE FAR LEFT AND LEFT
Kids' books and toys can be a source of colour and decorative inspiration. Plan shallow shelves: these not only ensure that favourite things are easy to get at but show them off when possessions are tidied away.

LEFT In a tiny nursery, it's vitally important to ensure that the area is kept clutter-free and tranquil. Pale shades will help make the room feel more spacious. In this baby's room, white walls, a painted floor and a contemporary wooden cot/crib look fresh and are easy to keep clean and tidy. Add one or two bright accent colours: here, a lime green upholstered Ernest Race rocking chair is a cheerful, comfy addition.

ABOVE AND OPPOSITE: In this nursery shared by twin toddlers, the design provides easy-care living at its best, with white painted floorboards, walls and closets. The cots/ cribs are on castors, so can be moved around for a versatile sleeping arrangement. Children need the stimulation of colour and pattern, too, so a giant map on one wall teams nicely with the possessions out on show.

OPPOSITE Children are sensual creatures, so pick surfaces that are practical but also cosy. This small family playroom has a sofa with a washable loose cover, funky fluffy cushions and a soft cotton rug. Kids' spaces must be planned with quick tidy-ups in mind. These simple wall-mounted wooden cubes are brilliant, as they keep clutter off the floor.

Casual living means adopting a relaxed frame of mind, and this is key when planning children's spaces. Viewed negatively, kids create a mess; viewed positively, they generate infectious energy at home, with a little chaos along the way. The casual family home is not about achieving perfection. It's about creating an environment in which everyone feels they can unwind. That means designing a home that is easy to care for, but one that still looks attractive when rooms are disordered. Apply the same principles to your kids' spaces. Their rooms should be jolly, uplifting places for chilling out, with a gentle nod to order.

Create a nursery that is soothing, yet with all the practicalities in place. Basic furniture includes a cot/crib, a changing mat on a chest of drawers, a nursing chair and hanging storage. The cot/crib sets the decorative tone: do you want to go traditional with a wooden, painted or metal style, or modern with sleek pale wood or colourful MDF/fiberboard panels? Stick to a pared-down design, and look for clever extras, such as an under-cot/crib storage drawer. Baby bedding must be easy-care, so go simple with cellular, stripy or plain cotton blankets, organic fitted sheets and a light quilt. Great nursery chair choices include a low Victorian-style slipper chair with a washable loose cover, or a comfy rocking chair.

Use alcoves for built-in closets and/or bookshelves, or buy a second-hand armoire and paint it a rich jewel shade like turquoise or purple, trimmed with funky handles. Add a mix of hanging rails and open shelves for toys and clothes. Don't put everything away. A sturdy denim container for teddies, wall-mounted canvas pocket storage and rainbow hooks for little dresses and coats provide a relaxed sense of order and inject personality.

ABOVE Second-hand school furniture and old office storage units are great choices for kids' spaces, as they are built to withstand wear and tear. Once kids know where particular items should be stored, they will soon get the hang of helping to tidy up.

Plain painted walls are sensible, but don't have to be boring! White is a blank canvas for bright baby things, but feels less clinical if teamed with a feature such as a painted floor, one wall papered in a whimsical print or lacquered spray-painted built-in storage in a contrast hue. Neutral paint colours like gull grey look tranquil; accent them with scarlet or leaf green. Enjoy mixing prints, from a blind/shade in vintage children's fabric to a dotted quilt and fleece blankets.

Once past the toddler stage, children need interactive bedrooms where they can play, so take an easy-come, easy-go approach to decoration. If you accept that you'll be repainting walls almost every year, it takes the angst out of picking a colour scheme. Go with the flow if your child wants sky blue, and ring the changes by painting a wall with

Add fun extras – some kids will love a ceiling-hung bed canopy, or a sea of Chinese paper lanterns, while others may prefer a hammock or tiny toy cars stuck onto the wall.

ABOVE It's unrealistic to expect a teen girl's room to stay pristine, but furnish it so that it's simple to keep tidy. Here, rows of hooks, an inexpensive junk-store bookcase and a capacious dressing table keep things in order.
RIGHT In this teenage girl's bedroom, a jumble of patterns, textures and colours make the bed fun. In place of matching bed linen, provide a selection of bedding, ranging from patchwork quilts to a retro floral duvet cover.

blackboard paint next year. Add fun extras – some kids will love a ceiling-hung bed canopy, or a sea of Chinese paper lanterns, while others may prefer a hammock or tiny toy cars firmly stuck onto the wall. Fit the window with a sturdy wood or metal pole, and experiment with simple curtains. For summer, high street stores have an endless supply of inexpensive tie-top unlined options, which can be teamed with black-out linings, or, using string, hand-stitch a jolly bed quilt straight onto the pole for a cosy winter option.

Encourage your kids to get involved with the casual living ethos. Make it easy for them to tidy up by providing low-level storage units with big, deep drawers, closets with sliding doors, sturdy

ABOVE LEFT Children are more interested in colour and whimsical accessories than a beautifully matched decorative scheme. This little girl's room is cosy, but it's also fun, because extras like the multicoloured canopy and a map-covered cabinet have been cleverly incorporated.

ABOVE RIGHT Add low hooks so that treasured possessions, such as dressing up outfits, are easily within reach.

stacking crates and open-cube storage that doubles as a display shelf. Junk stores are great places to find furniture that is already gently distressed, although make sure drawers open smoothly. Freestanding 1960s bookcases are often inexpensive – mount several along one wall and paint them all one colour, or organize toys into a low sideboard. Modern kids' furniture often comes in indestructible plastics, bright MDF/fiberboard or lacquered plywood.

The benefit of a casual approach really comes into its own when planning teenage rooms. Older kids need a comfortable space where they can enjoy privacy and experiment with new decorative ideas – they won't need much encouragement.

THIS PAGE AND OPPOSITE
ABOVE Some teens will prefer chilling-out space for hobbies; the bed is low priority. This room with a high ceiling has been fitted with a sleeping platform, leaving room below for the drum kit and entertaining friends. Use a mix of storage, from open shelves to a sideboard, to keep teenage detritus at bay.

Concentrate on providing flexible, fun elements that teens can move around and test out to create new looks. Strings of mini lights, old lamp bases teamed with Granny-chic silk lampshades or a battered anglepoise lamp are great lighting choices. As well as a bed and a desk, provide a low coffee table, beanbags or a divan/box spring bed on castors with a fitted denim cover, so they have an entertaining space for friends.

Taking a casual approach also means helping teens to personalize their rooms. Encourage them to delve into the remnant bin in a dress fabric department: floral, striped and plain squares can be stitched into quirky patchwork curtains. Let them paint their bedroom door or one wall a groovy shade, then personalize it with stickers, or 'wallpaper' a wall with posters. That's the fun part; teenagers might need assistance in keeping clothing and study materials organized. Perhaps devote a wall to open shelving: a grid of metal factory or catering shelves works well. Fashion-conscious teens will appreciate shoe racks and hooks for accessories.

Whether you have the luxury of a separate playroom or just a corner of the kitchen dedicated to the kids, don't try too hard to control the space. Make it a chilled-out zone that kids will make a beeline for. In a city home, bright metal lockers, found at office suppliers, look cool. Built-in closets with tongue and groove or old pine doors work well in a country home. Provide a tabletop for homework. A trestle table is an inexpensive option; staple canvas across the top for kids to doodle on. Office supply stores are a source of classroom tables with brightly coloured tabletops. However tiny the space, add comfy seating. Either upholster in a vibrant, large-scale print that won't show marks, or choose a cotton slipcover that can be machine-washed.

RIGHT An older teenager may find that a small room is all they need, provided there is space for a desk and a few treasures. Here, an all-white scheme and simple styling provides a blank canvas so that its occupant can make her own decorative statement.

boltholes

Whether a personal bolthole is immaculately ordered or gently chaotic, focus on decorative components that will promote peace and simplicity. In a small space, practical details must function perfectly, from folding doors to tuck-away chairs, so that this is a space that works effortlessly, day in, day out.

OPPOSITE Depending on the requirements of a hobby, it's possible to create a dedicated area for working in the corner of a living room. In this city flat, where the owner makes jewellery, a small table and angled lamp, teamed with original wall panelling, create an intriguing little bolthole.
THIS PAGE In this designer's studio, the casual mix of a trestle table and a plan chest provides an easy, vibrant working environment.

THIS PAGE On a half landing in this city house, a deep window seat provides the perfect spot for reading. There is extra storage underneath the seat, and a built-in bookcase opposite. Velvet cushions make it a luxurious place to escape to. The print is by Sean Scully.

LEFT Every busy household can use a spare desk or table. If the desk is for everyday paperwork or parking the laptop, equip it with an angled task lamp and a comfortable stool or swivel chair, and ensure that the tabletop is kept free from clutter so you can sit down, spread out and start working. Above the desk are watercolours by Bjorn Rosenberg.

BELOW Even the tiniest of backyards or rooftop gardens can provide the ultimate outdoor bolthole for a few precious moments of me-time. Add strings of mini lights and a few outdoor candles, and it will offer solace at night, too. This shady but luxuriant city garden is small, yet a bench has been placed in just the right spot to catch the sun.

However casual the rest of your living space, we all need time out and somewhere to retreat to for work, hobbies or down-time. A bolthole is just that: a private place to escape to. Our homes come in all shapes and sizes, so it's important to remember that a bolthole doesn't have to be big, but it does need to feel personal. Sort out the practicalities first – whether it's a quiet corner, a whole room or a converted attic, the space should be well lit, warm and comfortable. Only then can you concentrate on the decorative elements.

If you have successfully achieved a chilled-out mood at home, everyone will feel they can relax, in every room. But look for an unused corner that can be converted into a designated bolthole. A wide landing or a 'dead' space in the hall is an obvious choice. Is there room for a desk and a chair, or an armchair with an reading lamp, which will be a magnet for those wanting time out?

Choose furniture that makes a deliberate, look-at-me design statement. For a great desk, pick a retro 1950s design with colourful drawers, or for a romantic mood, try a marble-topped console table with delicate cabriole legs. In a neutrally decorated hall, a comfy armchair for reading could be upholstered in a bold, large-scale print. Consider adding a window seat to a deep-set window, piled with squishy cushions, and a built-in bookcase.

For a more organized bolthole, look out for areas in a room that can be converted into a mini home office. An understairs alcove is perfect: build

RIGHT In this compact mews house, the space under the stairs has been fitted with shelves and a worktop. When work is finished, folding doors hide it, and the chair is returned to the table.
BELOW A home office doesn't have to look utilitarian. With its cosy armchair, chandelier and reading light, this one is inviting and relaxed.

in a tabletop and add a comfortable stool on castors that can be tucked underneath, as well as shelves to hold storage. The casual home office won't be pin neat the whole time, so add sliding or folding doors so that everything can be hidden away when not in use. Fit the style to the rest of the room: glass doors will look smart in a city space, while panelled painted doors are good in a country home. Provided you have a table, a chair and storage close by, it's also possible to create a work zone for paperwork or sewing in the corner of a kitchen or bedroom. Blend the essentials with the rest of the room. Add flowers to a desk, and use jugs for pens or shallow sisal baskets to hold paperwork – you'll achieve a softer look.

If you do have the luxury of a spare room that can be transformed into a home office, keep the mood relaxed. The whole point of working from home is to benefit from a chilled-out environment, so forget about traditional 'office' surfaces like steel and plastic. Be imaginative with your furniture.

THIS PAGE A loft conversion is an obvious solution if you need to create a designated work zone at home. This desk area is tucked away at one end of a large attic room, which also houses a sofa and the TV. Quirky paint colours have been used to turn an empty space into a very personal, upbeat retreat. A dining table and a decorative cabinet have been snappily revamped with gloss paint.

LEFT AND ABOVE This home office is tucked away at one end of a living room. The essentials are all in place, including a filing cabinet and an adjustable chair. Yet their retro styling, and the fact that they are teamed with a wooden dining table doubling as a desk, makes the space feel laid back. Modern art by Elon Brasil and Duncan Pickstock adds a personal touch. **OPPOSITE ABOVE** If space allows, add a pair of stools or chairs to a desk so that two people can work companionably side by side. The shelves hold art by Braque, Corneille and Mogens Andersen.

A metal table painted in bright gloss paint, a black linen-covered tabletop on traditional trestle legs or even a scrubbed pine kitchen table are all perfect candidates. Instead of a standard filing cabinet, look for unusual storage, from an antique plan chest to a glass-fronted vintage display case. What matters most is that the storage is easy to access, and fun to use. Do invest in a proper adjustable office chair though. Get your local upholsterer to cheer it up with fresh, casual-looking upholstery in striped deckchair canvas or floral cotton.

A home office bolthole is all about creating a personal space. If you want a stimulating environment, paint walls in a vibrant shade such as strong lilac or warm olive green, but for soothing surroundings, choose grey, blue or stone. Small rooms look wonderful wallpapered in an unusual print; find a pattern that is cheerful and that will make you smile. Fit one wall with a giant pinboard, perfect for an imaginative mood board (interspersed with the occasional work information). Or use the walls as a gallery. Try amassing family photos, in black-painted cast-off

frames, or add a giant and exhilarating piece of art. This is your space, so make sure it pleases you!

If you regularly indulge in a specific hobby or craft activity at home – from screen-printing to ceramics – you will need a task-specific area for it. Are there any particular requirements? If ample daylight is required, house your workroom in an attic extension, or if the activity is noisy, consider a prefabricated home office at the bottom of the garden. Tailor your bolthole to your favourite activity, from building pigeonholes to hold artists' canvasses to having lots of open-topped baskets for fabric remnants, but keep the mood casual and not too workmanlike. Add a wipe-clean floor in rubber, but choose a zingy colour, or paint floorboards and walls sparkling white to create an inspiring artist's space. If there is room, treat yourself to two inexpensive tables: one for spreading out materials and another for paperwork and the laptop. And for those moments when you need to take time out and gather inspiration, add a cosy armchair or even a canvas deckchair. The secret to casual living, after all, is to work hard, chill out and love your home.

LEFT Treat your work space to the little luxuries you'd add to every other room in the house. A small vase of flowers, a scented candle and precious pieces, from your child's artwork to personal photos, will imbue a work zone with a relaxed air. **RIGHT** Provided there is space for the computer, printer and filing cabinet, the rest of a dedicated home office, like this one, can be devoted to eye-catching accessories.

source list

UK
FURNITURE
Appley Hoare Antiques
35 Long Street
Tetbury
Gloucestershire GL8 8AA
+44 (0)7901 675050
www.appleyhoare.com
Rustic French country antiques including painted armoires.

Cha Cha Cha
20–22 Avenue Mews
London N10 3NP
+44 (0)7739 517855
www.cha-cha-cha.co.uk
Original 1950s to 1970s furniture, lighting and textiles.

The Conran Shop
16 Sloane Square
London SW1W 8ER
+44 (0)20 7589 7401
www.conranshop.co.uk
Modern, sleek furniture, lighting and home accessories.

Fears & Kahn
www.fearsandkahn.co.uk
20th-century furniture, lighting and decorative objects.

Habitat
www.habitat.co.uk
Easy, simple and modern furniture, lighting and home accessories.

La Maison London
1 Old Oak Lane
London NW10 6UD
+44 (0)203 538 4310
www.lamaisonlondon.com
Antique and reproduction beds with handmade mattresses and bases in natural fibres made to custom sizes.

Loaf
+44 (0)20 3141 8300
www.loaf.com
Stylish furniture in key styles, from 1950s to romantic French at affordable prices.

Pinch
www.pinchdesign.com
Classic-contemporary armoires, sideboards, tables and upholstered furniture.

SALVAGE AND RECLAMATION
LASSCO
30 Wandsworth Road
London SW8 2LG
+44 (0)20 7394 2100
www.lassco.co.uk
Architectural salvage.

Retrouvius
1016 Harrow Road
London NW10 5NS
+44 (0)20 8960 6060
www.retrouvius.com
Salvaged furniture and materials.

Trainspotters
Units 3 and 4, New Mills
Libbys Drive
Stroud
Gloucestershire GL5 1RN
+44 (0)1453 756677
www.trainspotters.co.uk
Architectural salvage, especially 20th-century lighting.

Winchcombe Reclamation
Broadway Road
Winchcombe, Cheltenham
Gloucestershire GL54 5NT
+44 (0)1242 609564
winchcombereclaim.com
Reclaimed timber flooring, radiators, fireplaces and sinks.

KITCHENS AND BATHROOMS
Aston Matthews
141–147A Essex Road
London N1 2SN
+44 (0)20 7226 7220
www.astonmatthews.co.uk
Comprehensive choice of modern and classic bathroom fittings.

Catchpole & Rye
Saracens Dairy
Pluckley Road
Ashford
Kent TN27 0SA
+44 (0)1233 840840
www.catchpoleandrye.com
Cast-iron baths, showers and taps in antiques styles, plus flooring and tiles.

Drummonds
642 Kings Road
London SW6 2DU
+44 (0)20 7376 4499
www.drummonds-uk.com
Classic roll-top styles, marble washstands and taps.

CP Hart
213 Newnham Terrace
Hercules Road
London SE1 7DR
+44 (0)20 7902 5250
www.cphart.co.uk
Modern and classic bathroom suites, plus accessories.

IKEA
www.ikea.com
Wonderful range of budget kitchens and worksurfaces.

Plain English
61 Pimlico Road
London SW1W 8NE
+44 (0)20 7486 2674
www.plainenglishdesign.co.uk
Simply styled bespoke fitted kitchens in a choice of finishes.

The Water Monopoly
The Honey Factory
69-71 Scrubs Lane
London NW10 6QU
+44 (0)20 7624 2636
www.thewatermonopoly.com
Reproduction baths, basins and bathroom accessories, plus restored antique pieces.

PAINT
Edward Bulmer Natural Paint
+44 (0)1544 388 535
www.edwardbulmerpaint.
  co.uk
Natural paint range of more than 100 exquisite colours.

Farrow & Ball
249 Fulham Road
London SW3 6HY
+44 (0)20 7351 0273
www.farrow-ball.com
Quality, classic paint colours, from neutrals to bright and muted shades.

Little Greene
3 New Cavendish Street
London W1G 8UX
+44 (0)20 7935 8844
www.littlegreene.com
Contemporary and period paint colours plus wallpaper.

Paint & Paper Library
3 Elystan Street
London SW3 3NT
+44 (0)20 7823 7755
www.paintandpaper
  library.com
Inspired collection of paint shades plus wallpapers.

SURFACES
Alternative
www.alternativeflooring.com
Simple quality wool carpets and natural fibre flooring, including coir, sisal, jute and seagrass.

Fired Earth
www.firedearth.com
Stone, slate, and encaustic tiles, plus architectural stone and classic, simple wall tiles.

Stonell
87 Railway Road
Teddington
Middlesex TW11 8RZ
+44 (0)1372 860860
www.stonell.com
Stone flooring and surfaces.

Stone Age
Unit 3, Parsons Green Depot
Parsons Green Lane
London SW6 4HH
+44 (0)20 7384 9090
www.stone-age.co.uk
Limestone, granite, basalt, slate, travertine and marble.

Crucial Trading
South Dome, Design Centre
London SW10 0XE
+44 (0)20 7376 7100
www.crucial-trading.com
Large selection of seagrass, coir, jute and wool flooring.

TEXTILES
Cabbages & Roses
3 West End
Bruton
Somerset BA10 0BQ
+44 (0)1749 717095
www.cabbagesandroses.com
Striped, floral, plain and toile linens in fresh, simple colourways.

De Le Cuona
44 Pimlico Road
London SW1W 8LP
+44 (0)20 7730 0944
www.delecuona.com
Wonderful selection of linens in many textures and colours.

Ian Mankin
Worlds End Studios
Lots Road
London SW10 0RJ
+44 (0)20 7722 0997
www.ianmankin.co.uk
Natural fabrics at affordable prices, from linen to ticking.

Jane Sacchi
www.janesacchi.com
Specialist in antique linen and hemp sheets, plus French linen hand towels.

MacCulloch & Wallis
www.macculloch-wallis.co.uk
Huge range of classic fabric choices, including gingham, calico, seersucker, muslin and cotton lawn.

Malabar
www.malabar.co.uk
Strong and colourful furnishing fabrics in cotton and linen mixes, checks, stripes and plains.

Russell & Chapple
30–31 Store Street
London WC1E 7QE
+44 (0)20 7836 7521
www.russellandchapple.co.uk
Canvas and natural furnishing fabrics.

Whaleys (Bradford) Ltd
www.whaleys-bradford.ltd.uk
Vast choice of classic fabric choices, including calico, butter muslin, jute, cotton, linen and silk.

LIGHTING
The French House
www.thefrenchhouse.net
Vintage-style and industrial loft pendant lamps and classic lanterns.

Holloways of Ludlow
115–117 Shepherd's Bush Rd
London W6 7LP
+44 (0)20 7605 0667
www.hollowaysofludlow.com
French ceramic, industrial-style and prismatic glass pendant lights.

Original BTC
228 Design Centre
Chelsea Harbour
London SW10 0XE
+44 (0)20 7351 2130
www.originalbtc.com
Classic yet simple table, pendant and floor lighting.

BED AND BATH
Atlantic Blankets
1 Westcott House
St Pirans Road
Perranporth
Cornwall TR6 0BH
+44 (0)1872 573259
www.atlanticblankets.com
Lambswool, mohair, cashmere and aran throws.

Balineum
www.balineum.co.uk
Quality terry cloth towels, bath mats and cotton/linen shower curtains with inner linings.

English Eiderdown Company
englisheiderdown.co.uk
Bespoke eiderdowns made to classic designs.

John Lewis
www.johnlewis.com
Vast choice of good-quality bed linen, plus mattresses, bedding and towels.

Luma
98 Church Road
London SW13 0DQ
+44 (0)20 8748 2264
www.lumadirect.com
Organic cotton bed linen and towels, including cotton waffle blankets, linen and silk throws and hammam towels.

Marks & Spencer
www.marksandspencer.com
Stylish but easy-care bed linen and bedding basics plus towels at affordable prices.

Tempur
uk.tempur.com
Excellent choice of Tempur mattresses and pillows.

Toast
www.toa.st
Pure linen and soft organic cotton bed linen, hammam and linen towels, plus home accessories.

The White Company
www.thewhitecompany.com
Good-quality bedding, linen and towels.

ACCESSORIES
Anthropologie
www.anthropologie.com
Fabulously eclectic choice of home accessories.

Baileys Home
Whitecross Farm, Bridstow
Herefordshire HR9 6JU
+44 (0)1989 561931
www.baileyshome.com
Factory trolleys, converted apple-crate storage, industrial-style lighting and more.

Niki Jones
www.niki-jones.co.uk
Beautiful but simple furniture and accessories.

Oka
www.oka.com
Lighting, made-to-measure curtains and blinds, dining chairs with removable slipcovers and rattan baskets.

RE
Bishops Yard
Main Street
Corbridge
Northumberland NE45 5LA
+44 (0)1434 634567
www.re-foundobjects.com
Striped cotton fabrics, hooks, hardware and lighting.

US

FURNITURE

ABC Carpet & Home
888 Broadway
New York, NY 10003
(+1) 212 473 3000
www.abchome.com
Furniture, rugs, antiques, home textiles and accessories.

Bergen Office Furniture
61 Willett Street
Passaic, NJ 07055
(+1) 212 366 6677
www.bergenofficefurniture.
   com
Mid-century steel furniture, vintage and new desk lamps, old conference tables.

The Cherner Chair Company
www.chernerchair.com
Reissues of the classic Cherner chair design, plus tables and kids' furniture.

Crate and Barrel
www.crateandbarrel.com
Simple, easy-living furniture plus home accessories.

Design Within Reach
www.dwr.com
Modern furniture including tables, storage and sofas.

Hive
820 NW Glisan Street
Portland, OR 97209
(+1) 503 242 1967
www.hivemodern.com
Classic modern furniture, lighting and shelving/storage.

Pottery Barn
www.potterybarn.com
Affordable yet stylish furniture, plus great lighting, bedding and tableware.

White Trash
304 East 5th Street
New York, NY 10003
(+1) 212 598 5956
www.whitetrashnyc.com
Mid-century modern furnishings.

SALVAGE AND RECLAMATION

Olde Good Things
National Warehouse
400 Gilligan Street
Scranton, PA 18505
(+1) 888 233 9678
www.ogtstore.com
Architectural antiques, furniture, bathroom fittings and lighting.

Historic Houseparts
540 South Avenue
Rochester, NY 14620
(+1) 585 325 2329
www.historichouseparts.com
Vintage bathrooms, salvaged doors, sinks, tiles and lighting.

Sylvan Brandt
756 Rothsville Road
Lititz, PA 17543
(+1) 717 626 4520
www.sylvanbrandt.com
Reclaimed and weatherboard flooring, beams, and architectural antiques.

BATHROOMS

RH
www.rh.com
Beautiful, classic and simple bathware and furniture, plus linens and towels.

Vintage Plumbing
 www.vintageplumbing.com
Fantastic selection of antique baths, basins and kitchens.

Waterworks
www.waterworks.com
Bathroom suites, towels, and surfaces.

PAINT

Farrow & Ball
32 East 22nd St
New York, NY 10010
(+1) 212 334 8330
www.farrow-ball.com
Quality paint colours.

Zoffany New York
979 3rd Avenue
Suite 905
New York, NY 10022
(+1) 212 319 7220
www.zoffany.com
Attractive period paint colours.

SURFACES

Ikea
www.ikea.com
Pre-cut laminate or solid wood countertops, or custom-made in acrylic, stone or wood.

New York Stone
31–45 Howell Street
Jersey City, NJ 07306
(+1) 201 656 6200
www.newyorkstone.com
Granite, marble, limestone, travertine and slate.

TEXTILES

De Le Cuona
D & D Building, Suite 914
979 Third Avenue
New York, NY 10022
(+1) 212 702 0800
www.delecuona.com
Linens in a choice of muted or neutral colours.

O Eco Textiles
942 18th Avenue East
Seattle, WA 98112
(+1) 206 633 1177
www.oecotextiles.com
Eco textiles including linen and hemp upholstery fabric.

Kathryn M. Ireland
www.kathrynireland.com
Woven, ticking stripe, ikat and toile fabrics in linen and cottons, in fresh colours.

Perennials Fabrics
www.perennialsfabrics.com
Designer acrylic fabrics in sheers, solid colours and stripes.

LIGHTING

CX Design
304 Hudson Street
3rd Floor
New York, NY 10013
(+1) 212 431 4242
www.cxny.com
Classic lighting designs in Murano glass.

Vaughan Designs Inc
D & D Building, Suite 1511
979 Third Avenue
New York, NY 20022
(+1) 212 319 7070
www.vaughandesigns.com
Classic, contemporary and decorative lighting.

BED AND BATH

Stella
138 Reade Street
New York, NY 10013
(+1) 212 233 9610
www.stellatribeca.com/
Quality linens, towels, duvets and pillows.

West Elm
www.westelm.com
Stylish and simple bedding and towels plus mattresses and bedding basics.

ACCESSORIES

Anthropologie
www.anthropologie.com
Inspiring home accessories.

Michele Varian
400 Atlantic Avenue
Brooklyn, NY 11217
(+1) 212 343 0033
www.michelevarian.com
Industrial-style furniture, lighting and ceramics.

Ochre
462 Broome Street
New York, NY 10013
(+1) 212 414 4332
www.ochre.net
Vintage and organic textiles, ceramics, glassware and baskets.

Whisk
197 Atlantic Avenue
Brooklyn, NY 11201
(+1) 718 852 2665
www.whisknyc.com
Simple yet beautiful cookware, tabletop and flatware.

picture credits

Endpapers: The South London home of designer Virginia Armstrong of roddy&ginger; 1 The home in Copenhagen of designer Birgitte Raben Olrik of Raben Saloner; 2 The home in Denmark of Charlotte Gueniau of RICE; 3 The Sussex home of Paula Barnes of www.elizabarnes.com; 4 left The home of Charlie and Alex Willcock and family in West Sussex; 4 centre and right The home in Copenhagen of June and David; 5 left London house by Sarah Delaney Design; 5 centre The home of Charlie and Alex Willcock and family in West Sussex; 5 right The home in Copenhagen of June and David; 6 A family home in West London by Webb Architects and Cave Interiors; 7 A family home in London designed by Marion Lichtig; 8 A family home in West London by Webb Architects and Cave Interiors; 9 The Sussex home of Paula Barnes of www.elizabarnes.com; 10 The family home of Fiona and Alex Cox of www.coxandcox.co.uk; 11 The home of Justin and Heidi Francis, owner of Flint, Lewes; 12–14 The Sussex home of Paula Barnes of www.elizabarnes.com; 15 above The home of Justin and Heidi Francis, owner of Flint, Lewes; 15 below The Sussex home of Paula Barnes of www.elizabarnes.com; 16–17 A family home in West London by Webb Architects and Cave Interiors; 18–20 left The home of Charlie and Alex Willcock and family in West Sussex; 20 right–22 The family home of Alison Smith in Brighton; 23 above left A family home in West London by Webb Architects and Cave Interiors; 23 above right and below The family home of Alison Smith in Brighton; 24 Cathie Curran Architects; 25 The home in Copenhagen of designer Birgitte Raben Olrik of Raben Saloner; 26 The home in Copenhagen of June and David; 27 left The home in Copenhagen of designer Birgitte Raben Olrik of Raben Saloner; 27 right The home in Copenhagen of June and David; 28 left and above right A family home in West London by Webb Architects and Cave Interiors; 28 below right and 29 London house by Sarah Delaney Design; 30–31 The home in Copenhagen of designer Birgitte Raben Olrik of Raben Saloner; 32 above Cathie Curran Architects; 32 below The South London home of designer Virginia Armstrong of roddy&ginger; 33 Cathie Curran Architects; 34–35 The home of Malene Birger in Copenhagen; 36–37 The Sussex home of Paula Barnes of www.elizabarnes.com; 38 above left and below A family home in London designed by Marion Lichtig; 38 above centre Cathie Curran Architects; 38 above right The home of Justin and Heidi Francis, owner of Flint, Lewes; 39 The family home of Elisabeth and Scott Wotherspoon, owners of Wickle in Lewes, www.wickle.co.uk; 40 The home in Copenhagen of June and David; 41 The home in Denmark of Charlotte Gueniau of RICE; 42 above The London home of designer Suzy Radcliffe; 42 below left The home in Copenhagen of June and David; 42 below right The home of Justin and Heidi Francis, owner of Flint, Lewes; 43 The home in Copenhagen of June and David; 44 The home in Denmark of Charlotte Gueniau of RICE; 45 above left The home in Copenhagen of June and David; 45 right The home in Denmark of Charlotte Gueniau of RICE; 46 above left The home in Copenhagen of June and David; 46 above right The Sussex home of Paula Barnes of www.elizabarnes.com; 46 below A family home in West London by Webb Architects and Cave Interiors; 47 The South London home of designer Virginia Armstrong of roddy&ginger; 48 left London house by Sarah Delaney Design; 48 right The South London home of designer Virginia Armstrong of roddy&ginger; 49 left The family home of Elisabeth and Scott Wotherspoon, owners of Wickle in Lewes, www.wickle.co.uk; 49 centre and right The home of Justin and Heidi Francis, owner of Flint, Lewes; 50 left and centre A family home in London designed by Marion Lichtig; 50–51 Cathie Curran Architects; 52 The home in Denmark of Charlotte Gueniau of RICE; 53 above left Cathie Curran Architects; 53 above right The South London home of designer Virginia Armstrong of roddy&ginger; 53 below The home of Malene Birger in Copenhagen; 54 above left The home of Justin and Heidi Francis, owner of Flint, Lewes; 54 above right The family home of Elisabeth and Scott Wotherspoon, owners of Wickle in Lewes, www.wickle.co.uk; 54 below The home of Justin and Heidi Francis, owner of Flint, Lewes; 55 The home in Copenhagen of June and David; 56 above The home in Copenhagen of designer Birgitte Raben Olrik of Raben Saloner; 56 below left London house by Sarah Delaney Design; 56 below right The home of Charlie and Alex Willcock and family in West Sussex; 57 The home of Justin and Heidi Francis, owner of Flint, Lewes; 58 above The family home of Elisabeth and Scott Wotherspoon, owners of Wickle in Lewes, www.wickle.co.uk; 58 below and 59 The home in Denmark of Charlotte Gueniau of RICE; 60 The South London home of designer Virginia Armstrong of roddy&ginger; 61 The home in Copenhagen of June and David; 62 above The London home of designer Suzy Radcliffe; 62 below London house by Sarah Delaney Design; 63 The home in Copenhagen of designer Birgitte Raben Olrik of Raben Saloner; 64–65 The home in Copenhagen of June and David; 66 left The home of Malene Birger in Copenhagen; 66 right A family home in West London by Webb Architects and Cave Interiors; 67 above left and below The home in Copenhagen of June and David; 67 above centre and right The home of Justin and Heidi Francis, owner of Flint, Lewes; 68 above left The family home of Alison Smith in Brighton; 68 below left The home of Charlie and Alex Willcock and family in West Sussex; 68 right and 69 left The home in Denmark of Charlotte Gueniau of RICE; 69 right The home in Copenhagen of June and David; 70 above left The home in Denmark of Charlotte Gueniau of RICE; 70 above centre A family home in London designed by Marion Lichtig; 70 above right, below and 71 The home in Denmark of Charlotte Gueniau of RICE; 72 left Cathie Curran Architects; 72 right A family home in London designed by Marion Lichtig; 73 The home in Copenhagen of designer Birgitte Raben Olrik of Raben Saloner; 74–75 The Sussex home of Paula Barnes of www.elizabarnes.com; 76–77 London house by Sarah Delaney Design; 78–79 The South London home of designer Virginia Armstrong of roddy&ginger; 80–81 The London home of designer Suzy Radcliffe; 82 left The home of Charlie and Alex Willcock and family in West Sussex; 82 right London house by Sarah Delaney Design; 83 The home of Charlie and Alex Willcock and family in West Sussex; 84–85 The home in Denmark of Charlotte Gueniau of RICE; 86 The family home of Fiona and Alex Cox of www.coxandcox.co.uk; 87 A family home in London designed by Marion Lichtig; 88 above The Sussex home of Paula Barnes of www.elizabarnes.com; 88 below and 89 The home of Malene Birger in Copenhagen; 90–91 The family home of Alison Smith in Brighton; 92–93 The family home of Elisabeth and Scott Wotherspoon, owners of Wickle in Lewes, www.wickle.co.uk; 94 London house by Sarah Delaney Design; 95 The family home of Fiona and Alex Cox of www.coxandcox.co.uk; 96 above and 97 The family home of Elisabeth and Scott Wotherspoon, owners of Wickle in Lewes, www.wickle.co.uk; 96 below The home of Charlie and Alex Willcock and family in West Sussex; 98–99 London house by Sarah Delaney Design; 100–101 The family home of Fiona and Alex Cox of www.coxandcox.co.uk; 102–103 The South London home of designer Virginia Armstrong of roddy&ginger; 104 The home of Charlie and Alex Willcock and family in West Sussex; 105 The Sussex home of Paula Barnes of www.elizabarnes.com; 106–107 The London home of designer Suzy Radcliffe; 108–109 Cathie Curran Architects; 110–111 The home in Denmark of Charlotte Gueniau of RICE; 112 The London home of designer Suzy Radcliffe; 113 The Sussex home of Paula Barnes of www.elizabarnes.com; 114–115 The family home of Fiona and Alex Cox of www.coxandcox.co.uk; 116–117 London house by Sarah Delaney Design; 118 left A family home in West London by Webb Architects and Cave Interiors; 118 right London house by Sarah Delaney Design; 118 above The Sussex home of Paula Barnes of www.elizabarnes.com; 118 below A family home in West London by Webb Architects and Cave Interiors; 120 left The home in Denmark of Charlotte Gueniau of RICE; 120 right and 121 The family home of Elisabeth and Scott Wotherspoon, owners of Wickle in Lewes, www.wickle.co.uk; 122 The home of Justin and Heidi Francis, owner of Flint, Lewes; 123 The London home of designer Suzy Radcliffe; 124–125 The South London home of designer Virginia Armstrong of roddy&ginger; 126 The Sussex home of Paula Barnes of www.elizabarnes.com; 127 Cathie Curran Architects; 128 The family home of Fiona and Alex Cox of www.coxandcox.co.uk; 129 above left and below The family home of Fiona and Alex Cox of www.coxandcox.co.uk; 129 above right The home of Justin and Heidi Francis, owner of Flint, Lewes; 130 left The home in Denmark of Charlotte Gueniau of RICE; 131 The home of Charlie and Alex Willcock and family in West Sussex; 132 above The South London home of designer Virginia Armstrong of roddy&ginger; 132 below A family home in London designed by Marion Lichtig; 133 A family home in West London by Webb Architects and Cave Interiors; 134 The family home of Alison Smith in Brighton; 135 The family home of Fiona and Alex Cox of www.coxandcox.co.uk; 136 The family home of Elisabeth and Scott Wotherspoon, owners of Wickle in Lewes, www.wickle.co.uk; 137 The family home of Fiona and Alex Cox of www.coxandcox.co.uk; 138 top and139 Cathie Curran Architects; 138 below The London home of designer Suzy Radcliffe; 140 The family home of Fiona and Alex Cox of www.coxandcox.co.uk; 141 The family home of Alison Smith in Brighton; 142 The South London home of designer Virginia Armstrong of roddy&ginger; 143 The family home of Elisabeth and Scott Wotherspoon, owners of Wickle in Lewes, www.wickle.co.uk; 144 and 145 above The family home of Fiona and Alex Cox of www.coxandcox.co.uk; 145 below London house by Sarah Delaney Design; 146 The home in Copenhagen of June and David; 147 The South London home of designer Virginia Armstrong of roddy&ginger; 148 Cathie Curran Architects; 149 left The home in Copenhagen of June and David; 149 right London house by Sarah Delaney Design; 150 above The family home of Alison Smith in Brighton; 150 below The Sussex home of Paula Barnes of www.elizabarnes.com; 151 The home in Denmark of Charlotte Gueniau of RICE; 152 A family home in West London by Webb Architects and Cave Interiors; 153 above The home of Malene Birger in Copenhagen; 153 below The home of Justin and Heidi Francis, owner of Flint, Lewes; 160 London house by Sarah Delaney Design. Front cover: Judith Kramer, owner of webshop Juudt.com; the art of living; living and art. Back cover: The home in Denmark of Charlotte Gueniau of RICE.

business credits

Eliza Barnes Architectural Salvage and Design:
+44 (0)7977 234896
www.elizabarnes.com
Pages 3, 9, 12–14, 15 b, 20 r, 21, 22, 23 ar and b, 36–37, 46 ar, 68 al, 74–75, 88 a, 90–91, 105, 113, 119 a, 126, 134, 141, 150 a and b.

By Malene Birger
Head Office
Rahbeks Allé 21
1801 Frederiksberg
Copenhagen
Denmark
+45 3326 9620
www.malenebirger.com
Pages 34–35, 53 b, 66 l, 88 b, 89, 153 a.

Cave Interiors
www.caveinteriors.com
and
Webb Architects
www.webb-architects.co.uk
Pages 6, 8, 16–17, 23 al, 28 l and ar, 46 b, 66 r, 118 l, 119 b, 133, 152.

Also involved in this project:
Rick Baker Ltd.
The Workshop, Unit F2
Cross Lane
London N8 7SA
+44 (0)20 8340 2020

Woodland Commercial Ltd
292 Worton Road
Isleworth TW7 6EL
+44 (0)20 8560 0010
www.woodlandcommercial. co.uk

Solid Floor
69 New King's Road
London SW6 4SQ
+44 (0)20 7371 9551
E: fulham@solidfloor.co.uk
www.solidfloor.co.uk

Steyson Granolithic
Contractors Ltd
99 Sunnyside Road
Ilford IG1 1HY
+44 (0)20 8553 2636
www.steysonconcretefloors. co.uk

Fiona & Alex Cox
www.coxandcox.co.uk
Pages 10, 86, 95, 100–101, 114–115, 128, 129 al and b, 135, 137, 140, 144–145 a.

Cathie Curran Architects
E: cc@flexihouse.com
www.cathiecurran.co.uk
Pages 24, 32 a, 33, 38 ac, 50–51. 53 al, 72 l, 108–109, 127, 138 t, 139, 148.

Sarah Delaney Design
+44 (0)20 7221 2010
e: info@sarahdelaneydesign. co.uk
www.sarahdelaneydesign. co.uk
Pages 5 l, 28 br, 29, 48 l, 56 bl, 62 b, 76–77, 82 r, 94, 98–99, 116–117, 118 r, 145 b, 149 r, 160.

Flint Collection
49 High Street
Lewes
East Sussex BN7 2DD

+44 (0)1273 474166
e: sales@flintcollection.com
www.flintcollection.com
Pages 11, 15 a, 38 ar, 42 br, 49 c and r, 54 al and b, 57, 67 ac and r, 122, 129 ar, 153 b.

Marion Lichtig Interior Design
+44 (0)20 8458 6658
f: +44 (0)20 8458 7815
e: marionlichtig@hotmail.co.uk
www.marionlichtig.co.uk
Pages 7, 38 al and b, 50 l and c, 70 ac, 72 r, 87, 132 b.

Birgitte Rabens Olrik
www.rabenssaloner.com
Pages 1, 25, 27 l, 30–31, 56 a, 63, 73.

Rice
www.rice.dk
Pages 2, 41, 44, 45 r, 52, 58 b, 59, 68 r, 69 l, 70 al, ar and b, 71, 84–85, 110–111, 120 l, 130 l, 151.

roddy&ginger
e: Virginia@roddyandginger. co.uk
www.roddyandginger.co.uk
Endpapers; pages 32 b, 47, 48 r, 53 ar, 60, 78–79, 102–103, 124–125, 132 a, 142, 147.

June and David Rosenkilde
Stone-print lithographer and musician and producer
e: june@rehak.dk
Pages 4 c and r, 5 r, 26, 27 r, 40, 42 bl, 43, 45 al, 46 al, 55, 61, 64–65, 67 al and b, 69 r, 146, 149 l.

Wickle
24 High Street
Lewes
East Sussex BN7 2LU
+44 (0)1273 487969
www.wickle.co.uk
Pages 39, 49 l, 54 ar, 58 a, 92–93, 96 a, 97, 120 r, 121, 136, 143.

index

acknowledgments

Thank you Alison Starling and Leslie Harrington, for giving me the chance to write this book, an idea I first thought up while on a crisp, breezy New Year's Day walk by the sea.

Thank you, Polly Wreford, for taking such beautiful photographs, for totally 'getting' the idea of casual living, and for being such fun.

Thank you to Annabel Morgan, for talented editing, to Megan Smith, for a fresh design, and to Jess Walton, for inspiring locations. Thanks to my agent, Fiona Lindsay at Limelight Celebrity Management. And thanks to everyone for so generously letting us photograph their homes.

And thank you Anthony, Cicely and Felix, not just for your cheerful support, but for being the most wonderful example of casual living in action!